T0129534

CHARACTER, PLOT AND THOUGHT
IN PLATO'S
TIMAEUS-CRITIAS

PHILOSOPHIA ANTIQUA

A SERIES OF MONOGRAPHS
ON ANCIENT PHILOSOPHY

EDITED BY

W. J. VERDENIUS AND J. C. M. VAN WINDEN

VOLUME XXXII

WARMAN WELLIVER

CHARACTER, PLOT AND THOUGHT
IN PLATO'S
TIMAEUS-CRITIAS

LEIDEN
E. J. BRILL
1977

Raphael, *School of Athens* (detail), Vatican, Alinari.
Left to right (middle ground): Timaeus, Hermocrates, Critias, Socrates.
Socrates: "One, two, three — but, my dear Timaeus, where is the fourth of my guests o
yesterday ... ?"

CHARACTER, PLOT AND THOUGHT
IN PLATO'S
TIMAEUS-CRITIAS

BY

WARMAN WELLIVER

LEIDEN
E. J. BRILL
1977

ISBN 90 04 04870 7

CONTENTS

PREFACE

This book is an elaboration, after long abeyance, of the thesis proposed in the chapter, *Plato's Timaeus-Critias*, of my book (1961) and dissertation (1966) entitled *Questions of Intent*. I am indebted beyond measure to Prof. Peter Fraser of All Souls College, Oxford, and Indiana University for advice, encouragement and example over the past three years. To Professors Charles Kahn of the University of Pennsylvania and J. V. Luce of Trinity College, Dublin, I am grateful for reading the work at a nearly final stage. Prof. Walter Robert of the Indiana University School of Music, who encouraged me to resume my Greek studies, has been more of a support than he can have imagined through his companionship in the reading of Greek authors and the discussion of Greek matters. Needless to say, none of these expressions of gratitude should be taken as implying agreement with my thesis.

As I have had no official connection with Indiana University during the writing of the work, I am especially indebted to the several other members of its faculty and staff who have helped me from time to time and to the rich resources of its library.

My debt to my wife is immense.

Bloomington, Indiana, USA
October 1976

CHAPTER ONE

THE PRESENT STATE OF INTERPRETATION

In Plato's dialogues, the *Timaeus* and *Critias*, we have, if we disregard for the moment their rather puzzling disjunction, a continuous and far from simple dramatic composition. At the beginning of the *Timaeus* we learn that on the preceding day Socrates has described for four listeners, Timaeus, Critias, Hermocrates, and an unnamed fourth person who is today absent because of illness, the institutions and citizens of an ideal state, and has asked the four to repay this favor by showing him such a state come to life and by describing its citizens' words and deeds in war (17A-20C). Critias then tells a story of a war between ancient Athens and the vanished empire of Atlantis—a story which he heard from his grandfather, who heard it from Solon, who heard it from an old priest in Egypt (20C-26E). Because of the striking resemblance between the ancient Athenians of the story and Socrates's ideal citizens, Critias proposes that the three remaining debtors of Socrates use the story to repay him by assuming that his "best" city is the same as Solon's ancient Athens. Timaeus will first describe the creation of the world and of man, says Critias; then he, taking man from Timaeus for the peopling of his two cities and some superlatively well trained men from Socrates to act as the leaders of his ancient Athens, will tell his story in greater detail (25D-27B).

After this announcement of the program Timaeus performs his part of the task, and what we know as the *Timaeus* ends just before the conclusion of Timaeus's monologue (27C-92C). What we know as the *Critias* begins with Timaeus's closing prayer that his account has been accurate and that the gods will correct any of his opinions which may be inaccurate and with his transfer to Critias of the obligation to speak next (106A-B). Critias first attempts to convince his audience that Timaeus's task has been much easier than his will be, next describes the geography and institutions of ancient Athens and Atlantis, and finally, just as he reaches the subject of the war for the second time, suddenly ceases speaking (106B-121C). Thus we have a continuous and, in at least one respect, symmetrical drama from Socrates's opening question, "Where is the fourth of my guests of yesterday and hosts of today?" to Critias's last words and to our question, "What has happened to the second and third of the guests of yesterday and hosts of today?"

The would-be interpreter of the work—to refer to it provisionally as one—finds himself immediately faced with several anomalies: why does Plato begin with the mention of an unnamed missing speaker and who was he? why is there no mention in the program of a contribution to be made by Hermocrates? the juxtaposition in one work of a cosmological and physical treatise and a pseudo-historical legend seems incongruous; [1] the design of the whole, Critias telling his story both before and after Timaeus's monologue, seems clumsy; [2] the break between the two "acts" is unnatural; and the work gives the impression of being incomplete. These are only the most obvious anomalies which beset the interpreter; the more he reads and reflects, the more puzzles he sees.

In the long history of interpretation of the work there have been surprisingly few attempts to understand it as a whole, although the monologues of both main speakers have separately provoked a large body of commentary and conjecture. Efforts to elucidate Timaeus's intricate and often enigmatic account of the creation of the world and its creatures no doubt began shortly after the first publication of the work and have continued down to our own times. [3] Similarly Critias's story of ancient Athens and Atlantis has aroused frequent speculation, much of it such efforts to identify Plato's fabulous island with some known part of the globe as the recent contention that it was Thera, the volcanic island in the central Aegean, the excavation of which has revealed, beneath its volcanic deposits, the remains of a Minoan civilization. [4] But most of this exegesis has gone forward without much concern for the common sense rule of interpretation that a man's

---

[1] Wilamowitz, I, 599, 626.

[2] See pp. 3-5.

[3] Crantor of Soloi (c. 300 B.C.) wrote the earliest commentary of which we have record (Proclus, I. 76). Proclus's is the only important ancient commentary which survives; the most recent modern ones are by Taylor (1928) and Cornford (1937). For all surviving ancient, and for the more recent modern, commentaries see Cornford, xiii.

[4] Luce, 28-44, 135-59, 176. For the voluminous earlier speculation on this subject see Martin, I, 258-80; Gattefossé-Roux (over 1700 entries); Bramwell.

words should be understood with reference to their context—
Timaeus's monologue has been interpreted with little reference to
Critias's story or the dramatic situation, and interpretations of
Critias's story have been equally parochial.[5] If there is any of the
subtlety and complexity of true drama in Plato's work, then most
of the existing interpretation of it amounts to no more than reading
a drama for its thought alone without regard to character or plot;
and even this limited exegesis is largely confined to the thought of
one actor alone, without regard to that of the others.

The most important exception to this reluctance to consider the
work as a whole was the effort of Wilamowitz to deal with its
anomalies.[6] He concluded that the two dialogues as we have them
give us only a synopsis of the first, a hastily concluded version of
the second, and a synopsis and fragment of the third, part of a
monumental tetralogy. In its finished form Socrates would have
delivered a monologue on the ideal state in theory; Timaeus would
then have described the cosmos and the creation of mankind,
much as he does but with more care and polish near the end;
Critias would have followed with his story of ancient Athens and
Atlantis, telling it only once; and Hermocrates would have concluded the tetralogy by tracing the degeneration of society from its
ideal state in ancient Athens to the fifth century and by indicating
the way in which it could be restored to its lost excellence.[7] But
it was all too much for the tired and aging author, said Wilamowitz,
and so he gave up. Before abandoning the work, however, he wrote
a sketchy introduction to Timaeus's monologue which showed
what the whole might have been and was as much as to say, "This
is the way it was planned to be, but I must abandon it. Be content
with this summary." [8] Also he wrote out some of Critias's mono-

---

[5] In antiquity Severus judged the whole dramatic prelude to the *Timaeus*
unworthy of explication, and Longinus simply omitted 20 C to 27 A (Proclus,
I. 204). Chalcidius said nothing about the prelude, calling it "simplex
narratio rerum ante gestarum et historiae veteris recensitio" (p. 71). Porphy-
ry, Iamblichus and Proclus dealt with the story of Atlantis by transmuting
it into the names and categories of Neo-platonism (Proclus, I, *passim*).
Among modern commentators Wilamowitz and Rivaud (*TC*, 27-32, 119-20,
231-53) have been alert to points of contact between Timaeus's and Critias's
monologues.
[6] Wilamowitz, I, 592-9; II, 255-7.
[7] The origin of Wilamowitz's hypothesis seems to be Proclus's discussion
of the ἀπορία of the sequence *Republic, Timaeus, Critias* (I. 200).
[8] Wilamowitz, I, 592.

logue in finished form, and this fragment, found among his papers, was published as the *Critias*.[9] Interspersed with this reconstruction of his failure, Wilamowitz offered several explanations of it, allegations of incompetence, poor judgement, and fatigue, which it would be tedious to repeat.[10]

Such was the authority of Wilamowitz that this picture of a weary, incompetent Plato came to dominate, or where it did not dominate, to infect, most subsequent interpretation of the two dialogues, notwithstanding the fact that there was no conclusive evidence for it whatever.[11] That Plato ever intended to write a monologue for Socrates or that Hermocrates was to discuss a particular subject, were purest conjecture. But even Shorey, a scholar of more than usual common sense who recognized Wilamowitz's *Platon* as a "historical novel," nevertheless repeated as fact the conjecture that the introduction to the *Timaeus* was "an afterthought." [12]

If the tough-minded Shorey could make such a concession to conjecture, in the hands of a true believer the art of dismantling Plato's work and detecting his mistakes reached heroic proportions. Rosenmeyer (1956) reconstructed the evolution of the *Timaeus-Critias* as follows: [13]

(1) Plato wrote the whole Atlantis story as one monologue of Critias—i.e. the *Ur-Critias* consisted of *Timaeus* 20D-26E plus *Critias* 109A to end;

(2) he planned or wrote the *Ur-Timaeus* as a theogony only—i.e. it consisted of *Timaeus* 27C-69B and included no account of mankind;

(3) he wrote the brief dialogue of transition from the *Ur-Timaeus* to the *Ur-Critias* (*Critias* 106A-108D) which, since in it Critias implies that Timaeus has spoken only about the gods, ac-

---

[9] *Ibid.*; cf. Alline, 34.
[10] See especially Wilamowitz, I, 626.
[11] Friedländer, III, 383; Taylor *TC*, 101; Cornford, 8; Rivaud *TC*, 234; Gauss, III (2), 156. One might have wondered whether the intellectual and physical vigor and compositional skill to which the *Timaeus* attests were not cogent arguments for at least considering the opposite hypothesis; but the appearance of incompleteness was such persuasive evidence of inadequacy as to overcome all caution.
[12] Shorey, 2, 330.
[13] Rosenmeyer *PAM*.

cording to Rosenmeyer shows that at that time the *Timaeus* was, or was to have been, only a theogony; [14]

(4) he extended and altered the *Ur-Timaeus* to include an account of mankind (69C to end plus some insertions in the preceding part);

(5) the *Timaeus* now required an introduction which would pave the way for its discussion of mankind, and so Plato took the present *Timaeus* 20D-26E from the *Ur-Critias* for this purpose, but failed to change *Critias* 106A-108D to reflect the discussion of mankind added to the *Ur-Timaeus*;

(6) to replace the old introduction to Critias's story Plato wrote the present *Critias* 108E-109A and rather clumsily grafted it to what was left of the story;

(7) he abandoned the projected *Hermocrates*, which would have dealt with the ideal state;

(8) having, however, set his heart on a discussion of that subject, he invented the fiction of Socrates's discussion of it the day before, which he then prepended to the existing patchwork of Critias's prepended introduction plus the *Ur-Timaeus* plus the appended account of mankind.

Having made such a hodgepodge of the work, it is not surprising that Rosenmeyer is struck by "the inadequacy of the scheme as it has come down to us." [15]

If there have been few efforts to understand the *Timaeus-Critias* as a whole and most of these few at least tainted with condescension for Plato's senility, indecisiveness and general inadequacy to the task appointed for him by his interpreters, there have been none to understand the work as drama. Doubtless none would have appeared in any case after Wilamowitz's declaration of faith in his frailties (1919), but such a result had already been all but guaranteed by a chapter in I. Bruns's book, *Das Literarische Porträt der Griechen* (1896), devoted to what Bruns called the two trilogies of Plato's latter years, the *Sophist-Statesman-(Philosopher)* and *Timaeus-Critias-(Hermocrates)*. [16] Bruns distin-

---

[14] By the same logic Rosenmeyer should have postulated an *Ur-ur-Critias* without gods, since Critias implies (107 E) that he will deal only with mortal matters.

[15] Rosenmeyer *PAM*, 170.

[16] Bruns, 271-80. Merely by lumping these two "trilogies" together Bruns's book militated against any consideration of the *Timaeus-Critias* as drama, for it cannot be denied that the *Sophist* and *Statesman* are singu-larly devoid of dramatic interest.

guished this group of dialogues from those written in the "earlier, or realistic, style" by the following differences: they took place as the result of prearranged rather than chance meetings; for the most part the characters spoke after planning their speeches rather than *ex tempore*; the dialogues mirrored the organized and restricted life of the Academy rather than the unpredictable encounters of the streets and agora with all their attendant petty circumstances; conventional courtesy took the place of humor, banter, and occasional rowdiness; the speakers were usually anonymous or foreign rather than well known Athenians; the thought was no longer Socrates's but Plato's; the speakers taught Socrates rather than being taught by him; Socrates became a kind of presiding patriarch instead of a living, participating disputant; the "trilogies" were unconvincingly represented as being continuations of dialogues written in the old style rather than being autonomous; the speakers were puppets manipulated by Plato and not living characters drawn from real life and conversation. Bruns's explanation of all this foreshadowed Wilamowitz's: "It is quite understandable that, as with others so also with Plato, the time came when he thought that he had done enough, when with the passing years his artistic impulse grew weary. . ." [17]

Just as one could hardly be expected to look for Greek in Linear B after Sir Arthur Evans had pronounced judgement that Linear B could not possibly be Greek, so one would hardly look for art where Wilamowitz and Bruns had made such a crushing case against Plato's creative powers and the presence of art in his later works. And still one other circumstance, quite apart from the aspersions of learned Germans on his abilities, discouraged any suspicion that the text might yield an opposite conclusion—the apparent incompleteness of the *Critias* and, since we have no *Hermocrates*, of the "trilogy." Now it is seldom if ever remarked that, logically considered, the apparent incompleteness of a work can be due to either of two causes: it can appear to be incomplete because something interfered with the author's execution of his original intention—and therefore it really is incomplete; or, it can appear to be incomplete because the author's original or subsequent intention included giving to the finished work this particular appearance of incompleteness—and therefore it is really complete. No doubt

---

[17] Bruns, 280.

the number of subjects or situations to which the latter form is appropriate and the number of authors possessed of a temperament and capacity to choose and use it, are infinitesimal compared to the number of projected works which have remained incomplete for unforeseen reasons. And yet I can see no *a priori* grounds for concluding in the case of a given apparently incomplete work that either explanation is the correct one. The only proper diagnostic attitude is that either can be correct; the exegete must look for clues and see where they lead. But this skeptical view of apparent incompleteness has either never occurred, or never seemed likely, to scholars, and so the abrupt and seemingly premature ending of the *Critias* and the absence of a *Hermocrates* have played their part, too, in discouraging any suspicion that the *Timaeus-Critias* may be a unified and finished work of art.[18]

---

[18] For a study of some possible examples of feigned incompleteness, including an earlier essay on the *Timaeus-Critias*, see Welliver. See also pp. 34-37.

CHAPTER TWO

CRITIAS'S CHARACTER (1)

The one assertion of Bruns which, if true, would certainly eliminate the possibility of art and drama in the work, is that the speakers are mere puppets wagging their tongues while Plato speaks his thoughts—all of the other divergences from Plato's "realistic" style which Bruns sees are not necessarily incompatible with dramatic interest. But if the speakers have no character and no effect on one another, if each only opens his mouth to recite some portion of Plato's thought and then stands woodenly again when the recitation is over, there can be no drama. Hence it is crucial, if one hesitates to subscribe to the argument that the author of the *Timaeus* was senile, incompetent, and drained of his artistic powers, to inquire more closely into the questions whether there *are* any indications of the speakers' character and whether or not the speakers *do* interact on one another.

There are two sections of the work where answers to these questions are principally to be found, the dramatic introductions to Timaeus's and to Critias's monologues. In the first of these the answers are hardly noticeable, especially to a reader who is eager to get on to Timaeus's famous cosmology and if the second is not interrogated at the same time; but the second supplies rather telling evidence which, corroborating the hints of the first, lends substance to them also. Retrograde discussions of complex dramatic situations are apt to try the reader's patience and ingenuity, however, and so I will treat the evidence of the first section first, interpreting it in the light of the second and hoping that the reader, when he reaches that point in the following chapter, will not feel that I have been unjustified.

A remarkable aspect of the beginning of the work is the repeated and growing emphasis on Socrates's high regard for Timaeus in contrast to his other two hosts. The fact that in his first words he addresses only Timaeus is already a hint of this, but if stage directions are added to take care of some legitimate objections, such as Praxiphanes's criticism that a man to whom the scene was "manifest and clearly visible" (πρόδηλον καὶ τῇ αἰσθήσει γνώριμον) had no need to count heads out loud, the situation is clearer still.[1]

The courtyard of a house in Athens. Timaeus is standing alone in the center, looking up and lost in thought; Critias and Hermocrates sit together some distance away and somewhat hidden and are bent over in animated conversation, Critias doing most of the talking. Socrates enters; he sees Timaeus at once and says to himself, "One;" he looks around for his other hosts, catches sight of Critias and Hermocrates, and says, "two, three. . .;" he looks around some more, sees no one else, and finally goes up to Timaeus.

Socrates. But our fourth, my dear Timaeus, where is the fourth of my guests of yesterday who were to be my hosts today?

Timaeus. Some illness has befallen him, Socrates, for he would not willingly have missed this meeting.

Critias and Hermocrates, hearing Socrates, look up, stand up and walk toward him and Timaeus, and reach them as Socrates finishes the following speech.

Socrates. Then it is your task and that of these others (σὸν τῶνδέ τε ἔργον) to fill in the part of the absentee, is it not?

Timaeus. Certainly, and to the best of our ability we will not fail; nor would it be right after being entertained by you yesterday with such splendid hospitality if we—those of us who are left— were not eager to entertain you in return.

Socrates. Well then, do you remember (μέμνησθε) all the subjects that I asked you to discuss? [2]

---

[1] Proclus, I. 14. In addition to Praxiphanes's objection (from which, as far as we know from Proclus, he did not draw my conclusion) the following seem to me reasons for supposing that Critias and Hermocrates are not beside Timaeus during Socrates's first two speeches.

(1) Socrates is usually courteous. It would verge on rudeness for him to single out the one of the three partners who he thought could tell him about the fourth; if all three are in front of him, he should put the question to all three and let them decide who should answer it.

(2) If, all being in front of him, Socrates did choose to address his question to only one, then Critias, who is extending hospitality to some or all of the others (20 C, 26 C), would be a more logical choice than Timaeus.

(3) "σὸν τῶνδέ τε ἔργον" allows and, when compared to "μέμνησθε" in Socrates's next speech, even suggests, some spatial separation. Why not ὑμέτερον if all three are in front of him? For the use of ὅδε to refer to distant though visible things and persons see Soph. *El.* 4, 8, 11; Eur. *El.* 78, 107, 216. The opening of the *Gorgias* is a clear example of the stage directions which must be inferred in order to understand thought and action. It seems clear that Gorgias is not present at the outset but is at 447 C; therefore we must infer movement, presumably of Callicles, Socrates, and Chaerephon from the entrance to the interior of Callicles's house, where Gorgias is. In Socrates's speech at 447 B-C he first addresses Callicles, then Chaerephon, so that an actor's copy would show, before τὴν δὲ ἄλλην, "(to Chaerephon)."

[2] The goal of my translation has been to render the effect of the spoken word on the listener and thereby his impression of the nature of the speaker. Consequently I have tried to follow the literal meaning and word order of

In addition to making straight for Timaeus (if the stage directions are correct; in any case it is Timaeus alone whom he chooses
to address) Socrates both here and later (19A) calls him "my
dear Timaeus" (ὦ φίλε Τίμαιε), an epithet which he never addresses
to Hermocrates—in fact he never even speaks to Hermocrates
separately—and which, when he does once address it to Critias,
must be understood to be more ironical than friendly, since at
that point he is warning and by implication reproving Critias and
praising Timaeus (108B).[3] And in addition to these two marks
of preference Socrates conducts his recapitulation of the previous
day's discussion with Timaeus alone (17C-19B).[4]

The climax of Socrates's gentle distinction among his hosts
comes in his ensuing explanation of why he had gladly spoken for
them the day before. He wanted to see his superior citizens brought
to life and engaged in action against their enemies, he said; he
knew that neither he nor the poets nor the Sophists were capable of
doing this; thus there were left only such men as Timaeus, Critias
and Hermocrates who were capable; consequently Socrates gladly
discussed for them the subject which they wished to hear treated
in order, by obliging them, to induce them to speak for him on the
subject which he wished to hear treated (19B-20C). In the course
of this explanation Socrates praises the three men jointly and

the original as closely as possible and to make the sense no more clear or
consistent, though of course no less so, than in the original.
   [3] Cf. *Rep.* 599 D, "ὦ φίλε Ὅμηρε."
   [4] Note the laconic and accurate responses of Timaeus, often almost
identical with Socrates's question, e.g. (18 C-D)
Soc. εὐμνημόνευτον;   Tim. εὐμνημόνευτα:
Soc. μεμνήμεθα;   Tim. μεμνήμεθα.
Socrates reciprocates at 29D, twice using Timaeus's ἀποδέχομαι, and Timaeus
himself then repeats it twice in enunciating the supreme first principle
governing the origin of the cosmos. The pervading idea in this exchange is
that wise men accept what wise men say. Compare all this with Hermocrates's slight but revealing alteration at 20 C of the sense of Timaeus's
words (17 B; see p. 12) and with Critias's slight alteration at 26 A of Hermocrates's (20 C; see Ch. II, n. 18).
Socrates's apparent partiality for Timaeus is matched by Timaeus's
greater gratitude than that of the others for Socrates's favor of the day
before (17 A). Hermocrates, referring to Socrates's request, fails entirely to
mention his generosity (20 C); Critias, usually verbose, devotes only three
words to the matter ("σοί τε ἀποδοῦναι χάριν"; 21 A); even the absent fourth
speaker is described not as determined to repay his debt but as determined
not to miss the meeting. Both Hermocrates and Critias favor the grudging
style of appreciation (cf. 107 A). Compare Socrates's whole-hearted approbation of Timaeus's words at 29 D and 108 B and see *Rep.* 338 B.

severally.[5] They will know how to describe accurately the words and deeds of philosophers and statesmen, he says, because their "nature and training" (φύσις καὶ τροφή) have endowed them with the virtues of philosophers and statesmen. But when he goes on to praise them individually, we find that it is only Timaeus whom he unequivocally considers a philosopher and statesman: he is a citizen "of an extremely well governed state," has there "held the highest offices and positions of honor," and "in my opinion has achieved eminence in every branch of philosophy."[6] But "as to Critias, all of us know that he is no novice in any of the subjects we are discussing."[7] And "as to the nature and training of Hermocrates, that they are equal to these matters we must trust the report of many witnesses."[8] When we look carefully at Socrates's estimate of the three men, we can see that it expands the distinction already implied between his esteem for Timaeus and for the others to include a hint of their disparate abilities and that we would be about as justified in understanding Socrates to characterize them all and equally as philosophers and statesmen as we would be in believing that he considers himself one with the poets and Sophists.[9]

---

[5] Socrates first addresses Critias and Hermocrates by name here as he is about to praise all three as a group.

[6] Cf. *Laws* 638 B.

[7] These words are often understood as a high compliment to Critias, e.g. Taylor *Comm*, 49, but Proclus saw that they were only "ἔπαινός τις" (I. 70).

[8] The descending scale of Socrates's praise is also a descending scale of the reliability of the evidence: conclusive direct evidence ("in my opinion"), ambiguous direct evidence ("we know that he is no novice"), hearsay ("the report of witnesses"). The judgements on Critias and Hermocrates are phrased in their style of negative tribute (ch. II, n. 4), though with the difference that a negative tribute from Socrates is apt to indicate some lack of the qualities so negatively asserted instead of, as in the case of Critias and Hermocrates, a reluctance to admit them. It is a nice irony that Socrates should anticipate and adapt their negative style for his praise of them.

[9] The relations of the three with one another parallel Socrates's distinction among them. Critias and Hermocrates are cronies (20 C-D, 108 B-D, see p. 31); Timaeus takes no more notice of them than he must (17 A-B, 20 D, 106 B). Had the fourth speaker been present, he, too, would presumably have been included somewhere on the scale of Socrates's esteem (20 B). Timaeus's aloofness also from him suggests that he belongs with Critias and Hermocrates: the manner in which his illness is announced could hardly be more detached, and "τις" and "γάρ" intimate that Timaeus, rather than having seen or had news of him, knows that nothing short of illness could have kept him away (17 A). If this is the correct interpretation of the speech, it is one of extraordinary dramatic subtlety: Timaeus is not, as the reader first assumes, reporting a phenomenon (the illness) but in his very

Once the introductory distinctions between Timaeus and the
other two are finished, Hermocrates and Critias proceed to confirm their accuracy. Hermocrates at once offers a cheapened version
of Timaeus's expression of thanks to Socrates, substituting the
idea of the partners' having no excuse for shirking their duty for
Timaeus's "it would not be right." Next Critias provides us with a
glimpse of his nature and training which shows exactly what
Socrates meant in hinting that they are not those of the philosopher
and statesman (20D-21D).

> *Critias.* Listen, Socrates, to a story which is very strange and yet
> wholly true, as the wisest of the Seven, Solon, once said. Now he was
> a relative and very close friend of my great-grandfather, Dropides,
> as he himself often says in his poems; and he told my grandfather,
> Critias, as he in turn used to repeat to us in his old age, that great
> and marvellous were the exploits of this city in ancient times, the
> memory of which had been obliterated by the passage of time and
> the destruction of men, and that one was the greatest of all, which
> it would now be appropriate for me to relate both to repay your
> generosity and at the same time to praise the goddess, hymning
> her justly and truly, as it were, on her festival day.[10]
> *Socrates.* Excellent! But come now, what exploit was this which
> Critias used to describe, following Solon's report, as not recorded
> but really performed by this city long ago?
> *Critias.* I will tell you an old story which I heard from a man
> not young. For indeed at that time Critias, as he said, was very
> nearly ninety years old, while I was somewhere about ten; and
> it happened to be the Koureotis day of the Apaturia. The enter-
> tainment which was always customary took place also then for

first words is doing what he will do on the grandest possible scale in his
monologue, inferring the cause (the illness) from the phenomenon (absence).
Likewise the first words of Hermocrates (20 C) stamp him as a follower,
which he is (108 D); and the first words of Critias (20 D-21 D) accurately
forecast his role too (see pp. 12-15).

[10] For the genealogy of Critias see Appendix A. The *T-C* took place on
either the Greater Panathenaea (every fourth year) or the Lesser (all other
years), celebrated on the 28th Hecatombaeon (the Athenian lunar month
beginning with the first new moon after the summer solstice, June 20-21);
cf. 26 E. Either Critias was exaggerating the number of Solon's references
to his family or he has been unfortunate in the accident of the survival of
Solon's poems: only one refers to Dropides; in it Solon urges Dropides's
apparently wayward son, Critias, to obey his father; and its rude language
was adduced as evidence that Solon's family was low class; West, II, 133.
Critias is so intent on emphasizing his family's intimacy with the great
man that he never says in so many words that Solon told the story; Socrates
sets the matter straight: "ποῖον ἔργον ... Κριτίας... διηγεῖτο κατὰ τὴν Σόλω-
νος ἀκοήν;"

the boys, for our fathers arranged contests in recitation. Now of many poets many poems were recited, but the poems of Solon being at that time new, many of us boys chanted them. And one of the clansmen said—whether he really thought so then or was just paying a compliment to Critias—that it seemed to him that in other respects Solon was the wisest of men but that in poetry he was the most free-spirited of all poets. And then the old man—I remember it well—was much pleased and said with a smile, "If only, Amynander, he had not treated poetry as a sideline but had worked hard at it like others and had completed the story which he brought back here from Egypt and had not been forced on account of the discord and other evils which he found here on his return, to abandon it, why in my opinion neither Hesiod nor Homer nor any other poet would ever have been more famous than him." "And what was the story, Critias?" he said. "It was," he said, "about the greatest exploit, and the one which would be most justly considered the most famous of all exploits, which this city performed, but on account of the passage of time and the destruction of those who wrought it, the story did not last to our time." "Tell from the beginning," he said, "what Solon told and how and from whom he heard that it was true."

We could scarcely ask for a more telling vignette of Critias's training than this. Socrates has barely finished his aspersions on the poets "both ancient and modern" when we see the young Critias being indoctrinated with the importance and seriousness of poetry. Hardly have we left Socrates's summary of education in the best state, with its inevitable reminder of his proscription of most poetry in the *Republic* and especially of Homer's and Hesiod's, when we find the young Critias engaged in a contest of declaiming poetry and being told that if only Solon had taken poetry more seriously, he would have been as famous as Homer or Hesiod.[11] The grandfather's view of the matter is almost precisely the opposite of Socrates's: if only Solon had not felt obliged to deal with the problems of his city but had devoted himself whole-heartedly to poetry. . . , says the grandfather; "My dear Homer," says Socrates in the *Republic* (599D), "what city credits you. . . with having benefited it?. . . We say this of Solon, but who says it of you?" What irony there is in this scene of the grandfather's

---

[11] According to Plutarch (*V. Sol.* 29.6) Solon detested lying poetry and feared that lies in poetry would lead to breaches of contract. If the same evidence was available to Plato, it would have suggested that Solon, like Plato himself, detested much of Homer's and Hesiod's poetry and would not have desired a fame like theirs. For breaches of contract see pp. 18-21.

and the fathers' tributes to the deceivers of Hellas, as Plato considered them, during the Feast of Deception.[12]

In addition to the poets Socrates has just singled out the Sophists as a class unqualified in statesmanship and philosophy; hence it is a second telling feature of our glimpse of Critias's education that he received some corrupting instruction in rhetoric as well as in poetry. Here we can even see the instruction and the pupil's application of it at the same time. The grandfather liked to tease his listeners and savor his moment of glory by answering vaguely, when asked what the story was, that it was *about* something, and by pausing to let his listeners urge him a second time to tell it. Likewise Critias asks Socrates to listen to the story but then only hints at what it is about and pauses so that Socrates can urge him to tell it.[13] Like his grandfather, Critias is verbose; Socrates sums up in twenty-three words what Critias is unable to state very clearly in eighty-two. Both raconteurs are addicted to the use of superlatives: the grandfather, "the greatest exploit, the one most justly considered the most famous of all exploits;" the grandson, "great and marvellous exploits... the greatest of all." [14] And in one other element of rhetoric the grandson received some instruction: he suspected that one of his elders was lying in order to draw out his grandfather, and he observed that the lie was a useful tactic. Here again we can see his apprenticeship and its fruit almost simultaneously, for it is obviously impossible that Solon's poems could still have been "new" when his contemporary's great-grandson was ten years old—some fifty years, that is, after Solon's death at the age of seventy to eighty and therefore an even longer time after the appearance of most of the poems.[15] On the whole the instruction

---

[12] P.-W., *RE*, s.v. Apatouria.

[13] Cf. 26 C, where we find that the eager narrator continued to pause for urging from his audience and that young Critias took over the role of Amynander. Compare Timaeus's one businesslike pause at 29 D to see whether Socrates approves the premises of his investigation. Compare also the Egyptian priest, who does not break into narrative at the first opportunity (22 A), and his one pause (23 C) to see whether Solon, after having been told that he and his countrymen are ignoramuses, wishes him to continue.

[14] Note πολλῶν, πολλά, πολλοί, in one sentence (21 B). Note also that "ἀπεμνημόνευεν" (20 E), the tense of which Socrates follows with "διηγεῖτο," boils down to one time.

[15] Note the context of deceit in which the lie appears: the Feast of Ἀπάτη, the possibly false compliment of Amynander, the praise of poetry (of deceit, Plato would say). Why would Critias tell this particular lie? Perhaps to make his listeners believe that he was very close in time to Solon, as he has

in rhetoric was also appropriate to the Feast of Deception.

Besides poetry and rhetoric there was a little demonstration of hybris (this was more subtle than the other two, but we shall see that also here the young Critias proved an apt student): though Solon was reputed the wisest of the Seven Sages, the grandfather felt no hesitation in criticizing his judgement for having considered poetry a mere sideline. After this glimpse of Critias's training it is easy to understand why Socrates praises his abilities as a statesman and philosopher only faintly in comparison to Timaeus's.

As soon as Critias finishes his preliminary telling of the story which he says he heard from his grandfather and his grandfather from Solon and Solon from the Egyptian priests, he gives us our first clear look at his present character (25D-27A).

> What the aged Critias said, Socrates, following the account of Solon, you have now heard, so to speak, briefly; and when you were speaking yesterday about the state and the citizens about whom you were speaking, I was amazed as I recalled the things which I am now saying, perceiving how marvellously by some good fortune you agreed, for the most part exactly, with what Solon said. However I did not wish to speak right then, since due to the passage of time I did not sufficiently remember; so I decided that only after sufficiently recalling everything ought I to tell the story.[16] Consequently I quickly agreed to what you prescribed yesterday, thinking, since in all such situations the greatest task is the proposing of some plan appropriate to one's purposes, that we would be fairly well provided with one.[17] And so, just as [Her-

just made them believe that his family was very close to him socially. And why would Plato have him tell it? To stamp him as a liar from the beginning and to launch him on his demonstration of lying and deceit. It is possible that the lie contains the germ of truth that in 510 the recital of Solon's poems was for the first time in many years once again permissible with the fall of the Peisistratid tyranny (Taylor *Comm*, 23-4) or that a collected edition had just been published, but this would hardly occur to most readers.

[16] All the fuss about remembering (cf. 108 D, 112 E) is reminiscent of Phaedrus's protestations of his inability to remember Lysias's speech from one hearing, though he had made Lysias repeat it and had spent the rest of the morning memorizing it from the manuscript and had the manuscript with him (*Phaedr.* 227-228). Did Critias, too, have a manuscript of Solon's or his grandfather's story (cf. 113 A-B) and spend the night not recalling the story but memorizing the manuscript? Or are his too many protestations about remembering a smoke screen for inventing? Compare particularly 26 B-C with 108 D.

[17] Since Critias "did not wish to speak right then because I did not sufficiently remember," "ὅθεν ταχὺ ξυνωμολόγησα" is something of a non-sequitur. Throughout this paragraph Critias oscillates between the obscurity and clarity of his recollections. Perhaps the element of non-sequitur is

mocrates] said, yesterday as soon as I left there I began telling
them these things as I recalled them, and after leaving them I
got back more or less everything by thinking about it during
the night.[18] Indeed, as the saying is, how amazingly do the lessons
of childhood grip the memory! For myself, as to what I heard
yesterday, I do not know whether I could recall it all to mind;
but these things which I heard such a long time ago, I should be
utterly amazed if any of them has escaped me. With much childish
delight were they heard at that time; and, the old man eagerly
instructing me since I often questioned him repeatedly, like, as it
were, the images in an indelible painting have they remained with
me. Moreover, I told these others right after daybreak these same
things so that they would be well provided with themes along with
me.

Now then—and to this purpose all the foregoing has been directed—I am ready to tell the story, Socrates, not only in synopsis
but just as I heard everything. And the citizens and the city which
yesterday you described to us, as it were, in a fable, we, bringing
them here into the realm of truth, will assume that that city of
yours is this city; and the citizens whom you had in mind, we will
say that they are those true ancestors of ours whom the priests
described. They will fit perfectly, and we will not be out of tune
in saying that they are the very men who lived at that time. And
working together, each doing his own share, we will try to the best
of our abilities to do justice to what you prescribed. Wherefore
it must be decided, Socrates, whether this is a suitable story for
us or some other instead of it must be sought.

Socrates. And what one, Critias, in preference to this should we
adopt? For it is very well suited to today's festival of the goddess
because of its connection with her, and its being true history
rather than an invented fable is all-important. For how and where
will we find other stories if we ignore these? No, that would not be
right. You, then, must speak—and good luck to you—and I in
return for my talk yesterday must now keep quiet and take my
turn at listening.

We have here, obviously, a reenactment of the scene in which
the grandson saw the grandfather basking in the admiration of his
audience; with equal verbosity and self-satisfaction the grandson

---

induced by his shifting in this sentence from the labor of his recollecting to
his magnanimity in providing everyone with a theme.

[18] Just as Hermocrates's version of what happened on the previous day—
"immediately after our return to Critias's guest quarters, and even before
that, along the way," Critias introduced his story—becomes, in the version
which Critias attributes to Hermocrates, "yesterday as soon as I left [Socra-
tes]," so do the verbs of narration expand—εἰσηγέομαι (20 C), ἀναφέρω
(26 A), λέγω (26 C).

now repeats his grandfather's triumph as a raconteur.[19] And the grandson's triumph is perhaps even greater, for he is the discoverer and provider of the means of repaying Socrates and is therefore the benefactor of his partners. The most difficult task in any such enterprise as theirs is the formulation of a suitable plan; meditating incessantly since hearing Socrates's discourse, Critias has succeeded in finding this indispensable foundation for the partners' talks and has generously shared it with them; his, clearly, is the credit for making possible their satisfying of their obligation to Socrates and his the honor of command. Though Socrates may consider Timaeus the best of the trio, Critias obviously thinks otherwise.

In addition to demonstrating the effects of his training by claiming the major credit for the partners' ability to repay Socrates, Critias further testifies to its efficacy by a certain deviousness in his rhetoric. For example he plants the impression that he himself will be the first of the partners to speak: "Now then, and to this purpose all the foregoing has been directed, I am ready to tell the story, Socrates, not only in synopsis but just as I heard everything" (26C). Thus we and Socrates are not a little surprised to find in the next breath that not he but Timaeus will be the first to speak.[20] Why this sly tactic—does it serve to underline the role of Timaeus's monologue as a mere prelude and disappointing postponement of Critias's exciting and climactic full-scale narrative?

And then there is the sleight-of-hand by which Critias turns his story into the instrument for fulfilling Socrates's desire to see his city and citizens exhibiting their character in war. Socrates's city is marvellously like Solon's ancient Athens, Critias says at first, and then he proceeds by degrees to appropriate it: we will transfer your city from myth to fact; we will assume that your city is ancient Athens; in all ways they will correspond, and so we will not be out of tune in saying that your citizens *are* those very

---

[19] Note the frequency of the first person singular pronoun at 26 B-C, "ἐγώ. . . μετ' ἐμοῦ."

[20] Note that Socrates wishes Critias (the skeptic, see 107 B) "ἀγαθῇ τύχῃ" (26 E), reveals by "ὡς ἔοικεν" (27 B) that he had first assumed that Critias was to speak first, and instead of wishing Timaeus "ἀγαθῇ τύχῃ" assumes that he will begin by calling on the gods. "It has often been remarked that this introductory conversation, right down to Critias's last speech, might have been written for the *Critias* only. . ." (Cornford, 20). "ὑμᾶς" (26 E) does not show that Socrates is addressing his good wishes to all three; at 108 A he addresses Critias as "ὑμεῖς."

Athenians of long ago.[21] Obviously the city which Socrates describes could hardly *be* a historical city, but Critias, good Athenian that he is, takes possession of it by dubious means for his own purposes.

Immediately after Socrates's agreement that the story is a suitable one for repaying him, Critias tells him the program of talks which the partners have planned: Timaeus will first discuss the origin of the world and mankind, and then Critias will tell his story of the two cities in detail (27A-B). The implication is clear that before meeting Socrates the partners have come to an agreement regarding their respective contributions, and indeed the existence of such an agreement has already been implied in Critias's first words and will be confirmed in Timaeus's last. When Hermocrates asks Critias to tell his story for Socrates's approval, Critias replies that he certainly will "if our third partner, Timaeus, also agrees" (19D), which surely means that Critias's telling the story at that point was not provided for in the agreement or would in some way violate it. ("Certainly" (Δοκεῖ μήν), laconically replies Timaeus). And at the end of his monologue Timaeus relinquishes the floor to Critias "in accordance with the agreement" (κατὰ τὰς ὁμολογίας).

What were the terms of this agreement, which Timaeus rather pointedly observes and Critias asks permission to depart from no sooner than he has made it—for it must have been made between Critias's final narration of the story to his partners this very morning and their meeting with Socrates no more than a few hours, and perhaps hardly at all, later? [22] Obviously it should have provided for the sequence and topics of the partners' monologues: it must have stipulated that Timaeus would discuss his topic first (else why would Critias feel obliged to ask his permission to tell the story?), and one supposes that it also assigned to Timaeus the subject which Critias tells Socrates he is going to discuss.

Let us look at these two provisions separately. Early in the morning the three (or four) partners agree that Timaeus will speak the first monologue. A short while later, precisely at the point where either Critias or Timaeus should have briefly outlined the program of monologues and Timaeus begun his—for Socrates has just finished his recapitulation and said that he is ready and

---

[21] Critias continues and embellishes the metamorphosis at 27 A-B.

[22] Immediately after Socrates's speech of the previous day the four partners made a first agreement to comply with Socrates's wish that they represent his citizens at war (19 B).

eager to listen—Hermocrates breaks in and asks Critias to tell his story.[23] And in spite of the agreement Critias takes advantage of Timaeus's accomodating nature and not only tells his story—to which, and no more, Timaeus has now agreed—but expatiates on his own resourcefulness and generosity. In effect he exploits the change of order to step into the limelight himself, to take primary credit for the whole series of speeches, and to reduce Timaeus's story of creation to a mere prelude to his second and grander account of the war.[24] The conclusion is hard to avoid that at the very moment when Critias and Hermocrates were agreeing that Timaeus would speak the first monologue, they were in agreement between themselves (and the fourth partner?) that he would not, that they conspired from the beginning to pervert the stipulated order of speaking into the preparation of a triumph for Critias. How eloquent with laconic scorn, then, is Timaeus's closing remark that he will yield the floor to Critias "in accordance with the agreement."

Critias's and Hermocrates's part in the agreement is no less suspect with regard to subject matter than to sequence. A very short time before the partners' meeting with Socrates Timaeus agreed, we assume, to do what Critias says he will do, to describe the origin of the cosmos and mankind. Near the end of his monologue, however, he chooses one word which puts this assumption in serious question: he has now almost finished, he says, "the matters which I was ordered at the beginning" to discuss (τὰ ... ἡμῖν ἐξ ἀρχῆς παραγγελθέντα; 90 E). Ordered? [25] To come to an agreement is not to be ordered. What did the agreement specify as the topic of Timaeus's monologue and why does he say that he was "ordered" to discuss the cosmos etc.?

It is probably impossible to find a precise answer to the first of these questions; let us look, however, for an approximate one. The agreement specified either no topic or some topic: that it specified

---

[23] The maneuver of telling the story for Socrates's approval not only violates the agreement but is a little inappropriate: Socrates has just said that he is "πάντων ἑτοιμότατος" (20 C) to *receive* his feast of words, not to help decide in advance whether the cooks have prepared a good meal.

[24] Critias's scheme depends, of course, on his device of first telling his story "ἐν κεφαλαίοις" and then "καθ' ἕκαστον."

[25] παραγγέλλω appears two other times in the work (70 B, 108 B), both times in the sense of "warn"; but elsewhere Plato frequently uses it to mean "order," e.g. *Phaedo* 59 E, 116 C; *Rep.* 415 B. At 108 D Critias refers to his own assignment as "τὰ προσήκοντα."

none is unlikely on grounds of common sense (e.g., that the partners would hardly have met with Socrates without some previous allocation of subject matter). Specifying some topic, it specified either the topic which Critias announces or a different one: that it specified the topic which Critias announces (and Timaeus discusses) is unlikely, for in this case Timaeus should not have said "the matters which I *was ordered*" to discuss. Specifying a different topic, it specified one either totally or not totally different: that it specified one totally different is unlikely, because the risk would have been too great that so violent a change of program would provoke even Timaeus's accomodating nature to expose Critias's deceit. We can suppose, then, that the agreement assigned to Timaeus some topic less demanding than that which Critias orders him to discuss but not so different from it as to elicit charges of deceit against Critias.[26] Having agreed and, in the few hours or minutes remaining, prepared to discuss this topic, Timaeus suddenly finds himself called on, just before taking the floor, to discuss the origin of the cosmos and of mankind. A very pretty ambush indeed! [27]

In view of Critias's and Hermocrates's understanding of agreements it is instructive to look at the supposed origin of the Apatouria, the Feast of Deception at which Critias heard Solon's story and received some of his early moral and rhetorical training. The traditional origin of this feast was a celebrated Athenian victory won by the deceitful abuse of an agreement.[28] Melanthos, an Athenian fighting in single combat with Xanthos, a Boeotian, tricked him by saying, "Xanthos, you are violating the agreement

---

[26] Timaeus might have agreed, for example, to recount the descent of the story from the Egyptian priest to Critias (20 E-23 D), the gist of which he would have expressed in a few sentences, and then to tell what he knew of Egyptian cosmology, divination, and medicine (24B-C). He does in fact expound his—though not the Egyptian—understanding of these subjects; and such a discussion would have brought the priest's account to the beginning of the war (24 D), where Critias could have continued. It should also be remembered, however, that Timaeus and Socrates may be giving Critias and Hermocrates enough rope for hanging themselves (see Chaps. IV-VI), in which case Timaeus would not have exposed Critias under any circumstances.

[27] It is no wonder that we see occasional signs of extemporaneity in Timaeus's monologue; 48 E, 51 C, 53 E.

[28] Greene, 281. The legend varied in details; see P.-W. *RE*, s.v. Apatouria. Plato's family claimed descent from Melanthos on both the paternal and maternal sides; Diog. Laert. III. 1.

by coming with a partner" (παρὰ τὴν ὁμολογίαν, ὦ Ξάνθε, δεύτερος ἥκεις). When Xanthos turned around to see the other man, who was not there, Melanthos attacked and killed him. "Thus did the Athenians win by deception" (ἐξ ἀπάτης), says the scholiast of the *Timaeus*.

And so Critias, by ambushing Timaeus in violation of the agreement, is but following an ancient and honored Athenian tradition of dealing treacherously with agreements. Nor is he any less faithful to the Athens of his own day: his use of Solon's story to pay his own debt, his appropriation of mankind from Timaeus and the best men from Socrates, his vaunting, nevertheless, of his own generosity, his scheme for surrounding Timaeus's monologue with two of his own, his demanding from Timaeus a seemingly impossible contribution, all of these maneuvers have the distinct ring of Periclean Athens. She, too, turned on her "partners." She, too, boasted of her generosity even as she robbed. And she, too, knew how to twist agreements with the "partners" into edicts. Critias is true not only to the training provided by his family and clan but to that provided by his city as well.

Subjugating Timaeus, however, is a different matter from subjugating Melos. Timaeus's response to Critias's deceitful assumption of sovereignty gives Critias no satisfaction whatever, for he simply ignores it. In spite of the exemplary courtesy and gratitude which he has displayed toward Socrates (17 A-B), he never even so much as mentions Critias's story or his program or his generosity in providing everyone with a theme; he is totally indifferent to Critias's pretensions. As for the exorbitant contribution which Critias has demanded in the hope that it would humble him, it turns instead into the intended victim's triumph, marvellously applauded by his audience, according to Socrates (108 B). Small wonder that by its end Critias is furious.

CHAPTER THREE

CRITIAS'S CHARACTER (2)

Timaeus's monologue is a performance so brilliant as to condemn to anti-climax anything which follows it. This unexpected triumph provokes Critias to discard the trappings of generosity, courtesy, and comradeship which had earlier veiled his true nature and to expose the harsh and insolent and deceitful reality.[1] Let us begin with Timaeus's closing words (106 A).

> *Timaeus*. How gladly, Socrates, like one taking a rest after a long journey, do I now welcome my release from the journey of my discourse. And to the God who in fact came into being long ago, but has just now come into being in words, I offer my prayer that to whatever we have said correctly he will grant that it survives, but that, if involuntarily we have said anything wrong, he will impose the fitting penalty. And the fitting penalty is to bring him that is out of tune into tune. In order then that henceforth we may give a correct account of the birth of the gods, we pray that he will give us that most perfect and best of medicines, knowledge. And having offered prayer we give over to Critias, in accordance with the agreement, the next word.
>
> *Critias*. And, Timaeus, I take it; . . .

One cannot help feeling a certain rudeness in Critias's manner of taking the floor in view of the magnitude of Timaeus's achievement, his therefore large contribution to the partners' repayment of Socrates, and his evident exhaustion. But a more serious, though subtler, question of courtesy is raised by Critias's response. All of the partners' monologues, being repayments of Socrates's generosity, should be addressed primarily to Socrates, an elementary propriety which Timaeus twice observes at the beginning, and once at the end, of his discourse (27 C, 29 C, 106 A). It follows, then, that Socrates should have the first word upon the completion of a discourse in order to express his judgement on it and his thanks to the speaker. But Critias boorishly anticipates him and

---

[1] Compare Critias's behavior with that of Solon in Egypt, who is much pleased when the priest tells him, one of the Seven Sages, that he is an ignoramus, and wants to hear more (23 D). Cf. *Rep*. 409 C on the inability of the cunning and bad man to recognize the wise and good.

launches at once into his own really astounding exordium (106 B-108 A).

> What you yourself used at the beginning, demanding indulgence on the ground that you were going to speak about great matters, that same request I, too, now make.

Critias's first words are subtly prejudicial to Timaeus: Timaeus used a tactic (ᾧ ἐχρήσω); Timaeus demanded (αἰτούμενος) but Critias requests (παραιτοῦμαι). Also Critias's summary of Timaeus's exordium is deceitful: he nowhere said that he was going to speak "about great matters" (περὶ μεγάλων) and nowhere demanded "indulgence" (συγγνώμην).[2] He did, it is true, advise himself and his listeners to accept a merely likely account—providing it was no less likely than any other—on the grounds that accounts of mere likenesses can be no more than likely and that human beings cannot transcend this limitation on their powers of reason (29 B-D). But to call this a demand for his listeners' indulgence on the ground that he was going to discuss great matters is to twist advice and humility into begging and boasting, and principles of epistemology into tactics of oratory.

> I admit that the request which I am about to make is exceedingly presumptuous and more churlish than is proper, but nevertheless it must be spoken.[3]

How well Critias characterizes his request, and thereby himself! The request will indeed be presumptuous and churlish, among other reasons because at 107 E it becomes a demand—and deceitful too, as we shall see.

> For that your discourse was not a good one, what man in his right mind would attempt to assert? However, that the things I am going to say, being more difficult than what you said, require more indulgence, this I must somehow attempt to show.

In the first of these sentences Critias further reveals his dis-

---

[2] In his exordium Timaeus never uses μέγαλος with reference to his subject matter; "μεγάλου" (27 C) and "μέγιστον" (29 B) do not refer to his subject. At 48 C he explicitly pleads the magnitude of a task as grounds not for indulgence from his audience but for his not undertaking it. Note, however, the subject of Critias's story, "πάντων [ἔργων] ἓν μέγιστον" (20 E) and "περὶ μεγίστης... πράξεως" (21 D), and its importance, "μέγιστον ἔργον" (26 A).

[3] Cf. *Phaedrus* 260 D and *Rep.* 361 E where "more churlish [or harsher] than is proper" describes the speaker's attitude to something which he detests.

regard of the norms of courtesy: instead of praising Timaeus' discourse (as Socrates will do when he is at last given a chance to speak), he betrays his regret that he does not dare to find fault with it.[4] The two sentences taken together reveal the following thought: "I wish I could show that your discourse was a poor one: since I cannot do that, the only way I can get the better of you is to show that my task is more difficult than yours." Compare this with Critias's version of his relations with his "partner" which he expressed before Timaeus's speech—"Working together, each doing his own share, we will try to the best of our abilities to do justice to what you [Socrates] prescribed [yesterday]" (26 D)— or with the version which he will express when, well embarked on his story and again feeling himself in command, he has regained his good humor—"We [i.e. I] will tell you in order to share with you as friends. . ." (112 E).[5]

> For to seem to speak satisfactorily to men about gods is easier than speaking to us about mortals. For the inexperience and extreme ignorance of the listeners concerning whatever is of this sort afford great opportunity to the person who is going to speak about them; and we know what our condition is concerning knowledge of the gods. But in order that I may explain more clearly what I mean, follow me further. The things said by all of us must be, I suppose, imitation and representation; let us look then at the painters' portrayal of divine and human bodies with an eye to the ease or difficulty with which it convinces the viewers that it is successful imitation, and we will observe that in the first place we are satisfied if anyone is able to get even an approximate likeness of the earth and mountains and rivers and woods and the whole of heaven and the things that are and move in it, and inasmuch as we have no accurate knowledge about such things, we do not closely examine or criticize the paintings of them but tolerate a vague and deceptive sketch; but whenever anyone tries to make a likeness of our bodies, quickly perceiving its defects because of our close acquaintance with the subject, we become harsh critics of him who fails to achieve completely a likeness of every detail.[6] And you must observe that the very same thing happens in the case of discourses: regarding celestial and divine matters we are satisfied if what is said is even in the least likely, but when the subject is mortal and human matters, we examine what is said very searchingly. If in a speech made now on the spur of the moment I am unable to achieve a completely fitting representation, you must make

---

[4] See Ch. II, n. 4, above. Socrates speaks at 108 A-B.
[5] Cf. 20 B-D.
[6] Compare Critias's conception of κριταί with Timaeus's (29 D).

allowances. For you must realize that mortal things are not easy, but are difficult, to represent satisfactorily. It is because I wish to remind you of these things and claim not less but more indulgence for what I am going to say, that I have said all these things, Socrates. If I seem to demand this gift justly, give it willingly.[7]

What Critias tries to do in this main argument of his exordium is to gain a forensic advantage over his partner by turning to Timaeus's disadvantage the distinction which he had made in his exordium between the eternal model and the corruptible copy. He had said that the cosmos was modelled after an eternal, unchanging pattern, comprehensible by reason, and that accounts of this pattern (which he was not going to attempt) should be true while accounts of the visible copy could be no more than likely (28 A-29 D). But for Timaeus's figure of the maker of the cosmos who looks at the eternal forms and models corruptible bodies after them, Critias substitutes the portrait painter, who must at all costs get a likeness of his sitter, though it matters little how he daubs in the background. Then by a simple analogy between the painter and the speaker Critias manages on the one hand to vulgarize Timaeus's eternal forms, of which accounts should be true, into mere distant objects, of which any easy and inaccurate account will seem true enough; and on the other hand to ennoble Timaeus's shifting copy into a sitter for a portrait, whose exact likeness it is both all-important and extremely difficult to achieve.[8] By this sleight-of-hand Critias attempts to rank mortal subject matter above immortal; and by misleadingly associating Timaeus's discourse with immortal subject matter only, he attempts to rank himself above Timaeus.[9]

---

[7] Note that Critias reverses the order and alters the purpose of Timaeus's invocations. Critias invokes the favor first of men, then of the gods (108 D). Where Timaeus prayed that his discourse would be κατὰ νοῦν to both, Critias wants συγγνώμη from men, victory from the gods.

[8] Critias runs the risk of undermining the credibility of his own "true" story about the distant past by insisting on a speaker's opportunity for deception in describing distant objects. Rivaud (TC, 255, note 1) finds Critias's digression into artistic theory "a little long and foreign to the subject." But it is far more than a digression into artistic theory; it is, in fact, at the very center of Critias's purpose, the effort to outshine Timaeus. And it is the climax of Plato's delineation of his character.

[9] See Socrates's discussion (Rep. 349-50) of the just and wise man's refusal to vie with another just and wise man. This is the crucial point in Socrates's refutation of Thrasymachus's contention that the unjust man is wise and good.

As we observe Critias—his vanity piqued, his jealousy aroused, his scheme for ambushing his "partner" frustrated, by Timaeus's impressive discourse—as we observe him changing the occasion from a joint repayment of Socrates's generosity to an oratorical contest between himself and Timaeus, his deceitful nature emerges very sharply. In contrast to Timaeus, the true philosopher, he is the Sophist and orator skilled in making the better appear the worse. In his pursuit of this objective he degrades the discussion of divine things, for Socrates the most sacred of topics, to a golden opportunity for the orator to deceive his listeners; [10] he indirectly attempts that denigration of Timaeus's monologue which he has said that no man in his right mind would attempt, by implying that it was deceitful; [11] he misrepresents both Timaeus's and his own monologues by claiming more indulgence for his own on the ground that, in contrast to Timaeus's, it will deal with mortal matters, whereas in fact Timaeus's dealt with mortal as well as immortal, and his will deal with immortal as well as mortal; [12] and he lies outright in adding to the reasons why he deserves indulgence the circumstance that he will be speaking extemporaneously, since he has already said, when instead of begging his listeners' indulgence he was admiring his own resourcefulness and generosity in supplying everyone with a theme, that he had gone over his story with great care so as not to have to speak extemporaneously (25 D-26 C).[13] Having told his story three times in one version or another, not counting his nocturnal rehearsals to himself, having tricked Timaeus into an ambush from which only a superhuman command of impromptu exposition could rescue him, he is now

---

[10] Cf. 29 A, "ὃ μηδ' εἰπεῖν τινι θέμις."

[11] Critias's subtle disparagement of Timaeus's performance is a good illustration of an otherwise rather cryptic remark at 41 A-B: "τό γε μὴν καλῶς ἁρμοσθὲν καὶ ἔχον εὖ λύειν ἐθέλειν κακοῦ."

[12] Timaeus on mortal matters, 27A, 69 A-92 C; Critias on immortal, 120 D-121 C and passim.

[13] Cf. Menex. 235 C-D (the polished speeches which the funeral orators are eager to deliver "extemporaneously") and Phaedrus 228 A-E (cf. Ch. II, n. 16). It is, of course, possible that Critias, in his effort to get the better of Timaeus, is now going to embellish Solon's story and therefore truly to speak extemporaneously, if he has not already rehearsed the embellishments. But in that case he is violating his commitment to tell the story in detail "ὥσπερ ἤκουσα" (26 C). The most likely (and fitting) field for his embellishment is the appearance and institutions of Atlantis, which he does not mention in his summary (27 B).

reduced to pleading for indulgence on the ground that *he* must speak extemporaneously.

Consistent with these indices of deceitfulness are the several hints of harshness and greed in his nature. He is fond of the word χαλεπός (harsh, difficult)—he uses some form of it four times in his exordium.[14] In this connection it is revealing to compare his imperatives with Timaeus's: the latter are mild—"do not wonder," "we must be content," "it becomes us to seek" (μὴ θαυμάσῃς, ἀγαπᾶν χρή, πρέπει ζητεῖν; 29 C-D); Critias's are brusque—"follow me further" (μοι συνεπίσπεσθε; 107 B)—and his exordium ends with the supreme effrontery of demanding a gift—"give [the gift] willingly" (ἑκόντες [τὴν δωρεὰν] δίδοτε).[15] His repeated pleonasms, moreover, mirror his greed for more—celestial and divine, mortal and human, not easy but difficult, not less but more.[16]

If we add to the manifestations of Critias's nature so far mentioned the facts that Timaeus is a stranger in Athens and a guest in his home and that by Critias's own admission he is indebted to Timaeus for furnishing him with mankind, we have the unmistakeable delineation of an ingrate, a transgressor of the laws of hospitality, a blasphemer (at least in Socrates's opinion), a boor, a cheat, a perfidious partner, and a liar—great-grandfather of Plato though he be.[17] Thus we are forced to conclude that in the many

---

[14] With this and with Critias's harshness to Timaeus, compare the requirement for Socrates's guardians that they should be χαλεποί to their enemies, πρᾶοι to their friends.

[15] Compare Critias's "ἄκουε" (20 D) with Socrates's "ἀκούοιτε" (19 B).

[16] Pleonasm is an appropriate idiosyncracy for the unjust man, who does not scruple to πλεονεκτεῖν the just man (*Rep.* 349 C). In fairness it should be pointed out that Timaeus at 48 D says "πειράσομαι μηδενὸς ἧττον εἰκότα, μᾶλλον δὲ, . . . λέγειν." But where Critias's "not less" is aggressive and gratuitous, in that it assumes the argument, which no one has made, that the speaker discussing mortal matters deserves less indulgence than the speaker discussing immortal matters, Timaeus's "not less" repeats his own phrase at 27 C, and his "but more" amends it consistently with the statement at 48 B-C that no one has satisfactorily explained the elements.

[17] 20 A, 20 C, 26 C, 27 A; cf. Appendix A. It goes without saying that between a man of such a nature and Socrates there must be no less a gulf than between him and Timaeus; but since one passage in his exordium and one in Socrates's plainly suggest this antithesis, it may be worthwhile to compare them at the risk of laboring the obvious. In leading up to his characterization of his three hosts Socrates says that the poets and Sophists will be able to describe most easily those things among which they have been reared; but those things of which they have had no experience, such as philosophy and statesmanship, will prove very difficult for them to describe—"χαλεπὸν μὲν ἔργοις, ἔτι δὲ χαλεπώτερον λόγοις, εὖ μιμεῖσθαι " (19 D). In

decades from that far-off Feast of Deception to this day of the Panathenaea the defects induced and uncorrected by Critias's education and the society of his youth must have grown apace, perhaps without restraint in the latter part of the period, even as Athens grew without scruple or restraint after Salamis.[18] As he launches his overt attack on his partner, it is hard to see him as anything but the epitome of harshness and deceit and hybris, a condition rendered the more pitiful and ironic by the pride he takes in his own kinship with, and his story's descent from, Solon, the great Athenian sentinel warning against the penalties of hybris.[19] Instead of the justice and truth which he said befitted this celebration of Athena, he proves an adept of injustice and fraud (21 A); we can now see more clearly than ever that his speaking out of order was the symptom of his being out of order.

Critias's exordium he undertakes to prove that what he is about to say will be more difficult ("χαλεπώτερα") than what Timaeus has said. His proof is based on a division of subject matter strikingly reminiscent of Socrates's: considering himself to be the audience, Socrates posits one category of subject, philosophers and statesmen, about which poets and Sophists are ignorant but their audience to some extent knowledgeable, and another category, those matters of which they have had special experience, about which they are certainly knowledgeable and their audience quite possibly ignorant; considering men in general to be the audience, Critias posits one category, the gods and the heavens, about which both speaker and audience are ignorant, and another category, what is mortal and human, about which both speaker and audience are knowledgeable. It is clear that the situation which Socrates envisages is conceived with reference to enlightenment: in the first case the poets and Sophists will be ἄστοχοι and no enlightenment is possible, but in the second case (which, of course, is of no interest to Socrates here) enlightenment might easily occur. The situation envisaged by Critias, however, has nothing to do with enlightenment: speaker and audience are on a par in both ignorance and knowledge. What is on his mind is something very different (107 A-D).

περὶ θεῶν . . . δοκεῖν ἱκανῶς λέγειν ῥᾷον ἢ περὶ θνητῶν . . . ἡ γὰρ ἀπειρία καὶ σφόδρα ἄγνοια τῶν ἀκουόντων . . . πολλὴν εὐπορίαν παρέχεσθον τῷ μέλλοντι λέγειν τι περὶ αὐτῶν . . . τὰ δὲ ἡμέτερα ὁπόταν τις ἐπιχειρῇ σώματα ἀπεικάζειν, ὀξέως αἰσθανόμενοι τὸ παραλειπόμενον διὰ τὴν ἀεὶ ξύνοικον κατανόησιν χαλεποὶ κριταὶ γιγνόμεθα τῷ μὴ πάσας πάντως τὰς ὁμοιότητας ἀποδιδόντι.

Critias is interested only in winning the contest of "δοκεῖν ἱκανῶς λέγειν;" for him the goal is not, as for Socrates, Timaeus's "most perfect and best of medicines, knowledge," but victory in a contest of rhetoric.

[18] See Timaeus's remarks on defective τροφή, 87A-B.

[19] In the *Charmides*, where the family's kinship and intimacy with Solon is also emphasized (155 A, 157 D-8 A), Critias's grandson, the tyrant, is also vain, afflicted with envy, prone to recitation instead of thought, and given to lying (161, 162, 166, 169; see Bruns, 249-50). The three namesakes, five generations apart and stretching from Solon to the Thirty, make a genealogy to set beside that of the corrupt states in *Rep*. VIII-IX.

CHAPTER FOUR

THE REPAYMENT OF SOCRATES

Let us return for a moment to that request of Socrates which sets the other actors in motion: he wishes men who are both philosophers and statesmen to portray for him the behavior in war of the citizens of his best state. Critias nominates himself for the task: he tells his story, performs the sleight-of-hand by which Socrates's citizens become ancient Athenians, assigns Timaeus the task of providing a suitable preface to the full-dress narration of the story, and will himself portray Socrates's citizens-become-ancient-Athenians at war. All commentators have taken it for granted that, as both Hermocrates and Critias imply, this story would have satisfied Socrates's desire to see his citizens in action.[1]

A modicum of reflection, however, should suffice to warn us that this is not an entirely plausible assumption. Socrates wishes the limner of his philosopher-warriors to be a true philosopher, but Critias, if he is telling the truth in saying that the story he will tell is Solon's, is to be little more than a rhapsode, and if lying, is certainly not a philosopher. Socrates wishes the limner to be a statesman; but as Longinus rightly objected, if, as Socrates alleges, the poets cannot accurately imitate the ideal city because they have not experienced the life of a well governed community, then surely Critias and Hermocrates, citizens of Athens and Syracuse, cannot perform the task either.[2] These early warnings having now been reenforced by the realization that Critias is using Solon's story to get the better of Timaeus and by abundant proof that his nature and training are the opposite of philosophic, the assumption that he and his story will meet Socrates's requirements becomes completely untenable.

On the other hand it is crystal clear that Timaeus *is* blessed with a philosophic nature and training, is in fact the only one of the three so blessed. As to his qualities of statesmanship, Socrates himself says that he has attained the highest offices and honors in an extremely well governed state. On both counts he is the only one

---

[1] Proclus, I. 74 (cf. 75, 193, 197); Cornford, 20.
[2] Proclus, I. 66.

of the three qualified to do what Socrates wants (as Socrates's faint praise of the other two hinted at the very beginning), and yet his monologue contains no reference to the behavior in war of ideally endowed and trained citizens.[3] We have the paradoxical situation that what Socrates wants from a true philosopher-statesman he fails to get from the only true philosopher-statesman present but has been misleadingly asked to believe that he will get from a man who, by Socrates's own rule, cannot possibly be a statesman and soon proves to be the very antithesis of a philosopher.

This paradox is much more fundamental than the anomaly which has puzzled so many—that Timaeus's discourse, his masterly explanation of the cosmos and mankind, is only a digression between Critias's two narrations.[4] We can now see that this anomaly is Critias's doing, the result of his perverting the stipulated order of monologues to the end of his own and his accomplices' getting the better of Timaeus in a contest of declamation. But the paradox remains: if Critias could not have fulfilled Socrates's request and Timaeus, the only one qualified to fulfill it, does not, then the whole dramatic mechanism has misfired. The sole purpose for which the four men met not only was not, but could not have been, accomplished. This would be a particularly disgraceful failure for a work devoted to the investigation and praise of purpose on a cosmic scale, and we should do our best to avoid so unfortunate and unlikely a conclusion. The last passage of dialogue in the work, which follows immediately after Critias's exordium, suggests a surprising way out of the dilemma (108 A-C).

> *Socrates*. And why should we not grant [indulgence to you], Critias? And what is more, let the same be granted to the third speaker as well, to Hermocrates, for it is clear that a little later, when he has to speak, he will make the same request as you. In order that he may provide himself with a different exordium and not have to use the same one, let him speak assuming that he already has our indulgence. But I forewarn you, my dear Critias, of the temper of your audience; the poet who preceded you pleased it marvellously, so that you will have need of a really extraordinary measure of

---

[3] Except perhaps 54 A, where Timaeus says that anyone who can show that a better triangle than his is the basis of the construction of the primary bodies, will defeat him as a friend, not as an enemy.

[4] Hackforth, 7; Cornford, 20.

indulgence if you are to prove able to seize these things [i.e. this victory?].[5]

Hermocrates. Indeed, Socrates, you are giving me the same warning as Critias. But men of faint heart never yet set up a trophy, Critias; so you must go forth to your story-telling manfully, and, calling on Paion and the Muses, proclaim and celebrate the virtues of those citizens of old.

Critias. My dear Hermocrates, you are stationed in the rear with someone else in front of you, and so you are still courageous. But what a task this is, my labor will soon make clear to you...

Here Critias and Hermocrates appear to confirm still more explicitly what we have suspected from almost the beginning, that they are out to defeat Timaeus—for what other victory could this intended trophy celebrate? But more importantly, their military metaphor prompts us to identify their aggression with the very action which Socrates wanted them to represent. He wanted to see his citizens plunged into a "suitable war" (20 B); [6] for citizens of such superlative virtue surely the only suitable war would be a just war of self-defense; such a war requires unjust aggressors; and Critias and Hermocrates satisfy this requirement perfectly. In their treacherous attack and in Timaeus's victorious defense we have found exactly the defensive war in which Socrates wished to see his superior citizens engaged. Timaeus does after all contribute, and indeed preeminently contribute, to the satisfaction of Socrates's desire; his behavior under attack is Socrates's "best" citizens come to life.

In many ways the war forced on Timaeus tallies with what Socrates wanted to see. He wanted to be shown both the words and deeds of his philosopher-statesmen at war; in the war between Timaeus and Critias he not only hears their words but sees their actions and intentions vis-à-vis one another. Presumably he wanted to see citizens like his own, who are unmistakeably unhistorical, and not some such quasi-historical hybrids as Critias tries to

---

[5] Socrates here manages at last to praise Timaeus's monologue and at the same time recognizes Critias as the competitive rhapsode still vying for victory in a contest of declamation and tries to warn him that his situation is precarious. Compare Socrates's irritation at Critias's exordium with his enthusiastic approbation of Timaeus's (29 D). Plato only rarely uses παρα-λαμβάνω in the sense of "seize" (*Phaedo* 82 D, *Laws* 871 E, *Ep. VII* 332 B); in both Herodotus (7.211) and Thucydides (1.19; 4.16) it frequently means this. Hermocrates seems to confirm this sense in his subsequent exhortation of Critias.

[6] Cf. 19 C, "πρεπόντως."

invent; Timaeus, the actor who bodies them forth, has so far resisted all efforts to make *him* historical.[7] Socrates's guardians live in the Spartan style, needing only the barest necessities; Timaeus's laconic answers suggest that he, too, uses only the barest necessities. And as Timaeus in every way fits the part of the best citizen, Critias, the Athenian, and Hermocrates, the Syracusan, are marvellously attuned—perhaps even, as Socrates says, "uniquely among men now living"—to the part of the bad (20 B).

If the foregoing interpretation is correct, it is not Critias's version of Solon's story (though, to be sure, that has its own purpose) which would have satisfied Socrates's desire, had it been completed; it is rather Critias's treacherous attack and Timaeus's victorious defense which *do* satisfy him—Timaeus's utter indifference to Critias's claim to sovereignty, his magnificent minding of his own business, his triumphant response to the challenge suddenly thrust on him. Socrates sees the perfect citizens of his imagination come to life in a noble exemplar and win a victory befitting their education and training. We need search no further for the fulfillment of his wish.

---

[7] Cornford, 2. This is the more noteworthy in that both Critias and Hermocrates are so unequivocally historical and Hermocrates so prominent.

CHAPTER FIVE

CRITIAS'S FATE

Critias and Hermocrates, however, have not understood that Socrates has already been generously repaid; after all, the glory of the repayment was to be chiefly Critias's. Moreover, it is now clear that from the first their real goal was to get rather than give, to win a trophy with the help of Apollo Paian rather than to repay Socrates's generosity and pay tribute to Athena. Hence they persist in their "manly" quest for the trophy, not realizing that Timaeus has already set it up himself; but their evident apprehension suggests that they are quite aware that, for the moment at least, their intended climax has shrunk to the opposite extreme.

Of one danger, however, they are apparently not aware, namely the nature of their audience. "I forewarn you, Critias, of the state of mind of the audience" (τὴν τοῦ θεάτρου διάνοιαν), says Socrates, "how amazingly the first speaker won its approval" (108B). A prudent man might well have asked, "What do you mean 'of the audience,' Socrates? Is not an audience plural, or at least dual? Obviously I have not applauded Timaeus—quite the contrary—and Hermocrates has given no sign of doing so either, so you seem to be speaking only of yourself. It is not like you to inflate yourself into an audience. Who are there besides you in this audience which Timaeus has so pleased?" And Socrates might well have referred the question to Timaeus, since he identifies his audience both at the beginning and end of his monologue: "Calling on the gods and goddesses, I must pray that everything which I say meets, most of all, with their approval and, secondarily, with ours," he says at the beginning (27C); at the end he mentions only the divine audience (106 A-B). A prudent man might have understood Socrates to be warning him about his divine audience, especially if he had just shown himself rather disrespectful of it.[1] But Critias understands him to mean only the present company—"this audience here"— and doggedly sets about his task of defeating Timaeus (108 D).

---

[1] Cf. Socrates's frequent statements that a man plays his part before men and gods, e.g. *Euthyphro* 15 D.

Since Plato appears not to have completed the account of
Critias's and Hermocrates's campaign, we must now face the
problem, mentioned earlier, of the apparent incompleteness of the
work.[2] As was there maintained, the appearance of incompleteness
forces on the interpreter a choice between genuine and, as it were,
fraudulent incompleteness, the latter being a deceptive appearance
of incompleteness with which, for one reason or another, the author
concludes and masks the finished work. This is not an easy decision,
but it so happens that the *Timaeus-Critias* contains what might
be called a grand Platonic rule of exegesis for just this kind of
problem (46 D-E).[3]

> The lover of thought and knowledge must first search for causes
> originating in the reasoning faculty; but such causes as come into
> being from things set in motion by other things and themselves of
> necessity setting other things in motion, these must be sought
> only secondarily ... We must distinguish causes which work with
> intelligent purpose to produce what is beautiful and good from
> those which, lacking reason, always work by chance and without
> order.

With regard to the problem of incompleteness in general this is a
forceful argument for searching for evidence of feigned incompleteness as against hastily assuming the operation of unpredictable
extraneous causes, especially in the case of such subtle and purpose-
ful writers as Plato. With regard to the *Timaeus-Critias* in particular the argument is even stronger, for it is clearly natural and
reasonable to proceed to the exegesis of a work by following any
principle of exegesis which it seems to urge.

Not only does this work contain a principle for its own exegesis,
but among likely cases of feigned incompleteness with which I am
familiar it is unique in its frequent references to the subject of
incompleteness.[4] "One, two, three, but where is the fourth of my
hosts?" says Socrates in the opening words. When he observes
that the survivors will have to supply the part of the missing
fourth, Timaeus answers that they will do their best "to leave
nothing out." At 19 B Socrates asks Timaeus if his recapitulation is
complete, and Timaeus answers that it is, but 20 B shows that in
one respect it was not. "If only... [Solon] had finished the story

---

[2] See p. 6.
[3] Cf. 68 E.
[4] Cf. Ch. I, n. 18.

which he brought back from Egypt and had not been forced to lay it aside. . . ," says Critias the elder (21 C). When Critias the younger announces the program of the partners' speeches, he succinctly states the content of Timaeus's, grows verbosely vague about his own, and omits entirely to mention Hermocrates (27 A-B).[5] "Completely and brilliantly (τελέως τε καὶ λαμπρῶς), it seems, am I about to be repaid with a feast of speeches," says Socrates with his usual perception (27 B). Obviously the idea of incompleteness was much in Plato's mind at the outset.

Critias's program of speeches is remarkable not only for its promise of one-third less than we have been led to expect that we shall get, but for its accurate forecast of what at the end we find we have gotten. He tells us how Timaeus's monologue will begin and end, and thus it does begin and end. His prospect of the beginning of his own proves a little high-flown, it is true, for he says nothing there about taking men from Timaeus and Socrates and, like Solon, making them citizens; this foretaste of what his prologue would have been had he not had to attack Timaeus instead, is both a product of his imperial euphoria, which has been a little dampened by the time his turn comes to speak, and the result of his need to transmute Socrates's citizens into his ancient Athenians. But in essence he simply says that he will speak about Athenian citizens, and this, as we shall see, is a better description of his whole monologue than even he realizes. He fails to mention Hermocrates and Hermocrates fails to speak. Arrived at the end of the work we can see that we have had from the beginning a surprisingly accurate forecast of its entire contents.[6]

In still another respect there is an element of completion in the ending of the work. At the beginning Critias has told the whole story of the two cities, not only through their war but even to their final dissolution. In his monologue he fully describes what he has omitted from his summary account, the founding and

---

[5] Note "ἀποτετελεχέναι," 108 D.

[6] This extraordinary statement of the program—a stingy but accurate synopsis of Timaeus's complete discourse, a pretentious but incomplete synopsis of Critias's own, no mention of Hermocrates's—corresponds so closely to what actually takes place in the work as to constitute by itself the virtual proof of Plato's premeditation of the design as we have it, including the appearance of incompleteness. The descending order of completeness is parallel to the descending order of Socrates's praise of the three men (19 E-20 B).

geography and customs of the cities. Then, in his last words, he reveals for the first time the cause of the war: the Atlantids became drunk with hybris, God saw that they were in trouble and needed to be cured by punishment, therefore he contrived to lure them into the war with Athens which resulted in their crushing defeat. Only with these last words of Critias can we fully understand the story of which we have previously been given every other necessary particular; his last words close the circle with the final cause.[7]

Thus, to recapitulate, Plato hints copiously at the beginning that he is interested in the phenomenon of apparent incompleteness, he gives us an apparently premature ending at a point, however, where both Critias's program of speeches and his story are in a way completed, and he includes in his work an eloquent admonition to search for purpose rather than accepting chance as the explanation of phenomena. Can we escape the obligation to search for purpose in the seemingly fortuitous ending? [8]

Critias unexpectedly and abruptly ceases speaking at the end of the following words:

> The god of gods, Zeus, ruling by law, reflecting, since he is able to perceive such things, how this fine people [the Atlantids] had gotten into a wretched state, wishing to punish them so that, recalled to their senses, they might strike a truer note, assembled all of the gods in their most honored dwelling, which, standing at the middle of the whole cosmos, surveys everything which partakes of generation; and, having assembled them, he said.

Now Critias has also gotten into a wretched state, as we have seen. Vis-à-vis the architect of the cosmos, in whom, according to Timaeus, "no envy ever arises concerning anything," the envious rival of Timaeus has indeed gotten into the most wretched state

---

[7] Note also that Socrates in his recapitulation of his previous day's discourse reveals his purpose only at the end (20 B).

[8] The apparently incomplete "trilogy" Sophist, Statesman, (Philosopher), seems to me to be of little if any use in interpreting the T-C: the resemblance is only superficial. The former has virtually no dramatic elements—no character (except, in a lifeless way, young versus old), no plot, no ἔργα. The device of dialogue is perfunctory: the speakers really are, as Bruns said, mere puppets for Plato's didactic thought. Where the T-C consists of conversations which display the actors' character and of stories, the S-S-(Ph) deals with bloodless types. There is nothing in the latter similar to the numerous hints of subtle dramatic design in the T-C, and no such rich and ironic relation between the absence of the Philosopher and the two preceding dialogues as exists between the incompleteness of the Critias and absence of the Hermocrates on the one hand and the T-C on the other.

imaginable (29 D-E).⁹ And at this point in his campaign against Timaeus he has arrived at a particularly delicate juncture: previously he has said that men's ignorance of the gods offers a great opportunity to the speaker who discusses them; here he is on the point of doing nothing less than quoting Zeus, of seizing his golden opportunity. Here also he has just revealed that Zeus punishes those who have gotten into so wretched a state as his. Need we doubt what happens to him as he takes up this most exposed and vulnerable position in his campaign? Does he not receive that same treatment which Timaeus requests for anything he may have said which is out of tune (παρὰ μέλος)—"to bring into tune him who is out of tune" (τὸν πλημμελοῦντα ἐμμελῆ ποιεῖν; 106 B)—and which Zeus is about to inflict on the Atlantids in order to make them "more in tune" (ἐμμελέστεροι)? ¹⁰

There is, of course, room for speculation as to details; did he, like his words, vanish and leave not a rack behind? Perhaps not— or at least not right away. We have at the other end of the work an excellent precedent in the matter of the unexpected failure of a speaker: "Some illness has befallen him," says Timaeus of the missing fourth partner. If one were to follow this hint, he would be inclined to ascribe also Critias's sudden silence to a sudden illness; and judging from Critias's moral state at this point, the illness must have been serious, though perhaps not immediately fatal.

From this reconstruction of the plot there arise two corollary questions. What of that fourth partner—was his illness punitive, too? Was he, being stricken sooner than Critias, even more wicked than Critias, perhaps the arch conspirator who instigated the

---

⁹ Note the Egyptian priest's "φθόνος οὐδείς" (23 D). For proof that the divine ἀρχή of "no envy" is an important principle for disputants, see 54 A; Critias's style of disputation is the reverse of this. Cf. 90 and *Gorg.* 507-8 for man's need to attune himself to the harmony of the cosmos.

¹⁰ Note that Critias's removal from the scene would be consistent with both Socrates's political, and Timaeus's individual eschatology. In Socrates's ideal state the bad are cleverly sorted from the good and quietly sent offstage in such a way that almost everyone assumes the agent to be chance (18 D). In Timaeus's cosmos good men are rewarded with eternal blessedness while the bad and unphilosophic are removed to the animal orders (90 B-92 C). For other examples of sudden divine punishment for dishonest or impious speech (Stesichorus, Homer) see *Phaedr.* 243 A. Critias's punishment at the end of the work would also be consistent with Plato's conclusion of Timaeus's monologue, of the *Republic* (608-21, cf. 330 E, 498 C-D), and of the *Gorgias* (523-26, cf. 507 D) with figures or myths of punishment after death (cf. *Phaedo* 63 C).

attack on Timaeus? Who was he? Secondly, what should we make of the remarkable similarity and coincidence in the fate of Critias and that of Atlantis? Insolent, swollen Atlantis was lured by Zeus to attack modest little Athens and met her doom. Insolent Critias, the big-city aristocrat, along with Hermocrates and perhaps the fourth partner, attacked the modest visitor from the little Italian city and met his doom just as he revealed the cause of Atlantis's. Is there some strange kinship between Critias and his Atlantis; and was he, too, lured to the attack by someone who perceived his wretched state in order that he, too, might strike a truer note? But these questions must await consideration of his tale of the two cities.

CHAPTER SIX

THE TRUTH OF CRITIAS'S STORY

The story of ancient Athens is called true at two points: in Critias's first words he says it is "an entirely true story" (λόγου παντάπασί γε μὴν ἀληθοῦς; 20 D), and when Socrates assents to its use, he says that the fact that it is a "true story" (ἀληθινὸν λόγον; 26 E) is all-important. Both of these assertions, however, are subject to some qualification from the context. Without going so far as to say that nothing which Critias says is reliable (for there are always the spirits of Solon and Egyptian wisdom somewhere behind him), still "entirely" (παντάπασι) betrays that fascination with the superlative which is peculiar to Critias.[1] And when Socrates calls the story true, he is simply repeating Critias's assertion and courteously agreeing with the invidious distinction which Critias has just implied between Socrates's mere fable of the day before and Critias's true story (26 C). Nevertheless the authority of Egypt and Solon is a stern warning against assuming the story to be entirely false. In some sense it must be true; in some way it must fit some history.

There is, of course, no history which it literally fits. It ends with the destruction of both societies by cataclysm: in one day and night of floods and earthquakes all the Athenian soldiers disappeared beneath the earth and the island of Atlantis sank into the sea. No sunken island lies beneath the Atlantic, however, and geologists tell us that none could have lain there for countless millenia. Lacking this, those who for one reason or another believe or hope that Plato had in mind some specific place when he drew Atlantis, grasp at the straws of stray resemblances. The most recent of these has been the evidence of the destruction of Thera, and perhaps of the ending of all Minoan civilization, by volcanic eruption; but like earlier candidates, Minoan civilization is not a very good fit.[2] Its particular and most obvious defects are the

---

[1] It must be remembered, moreover, that Critias in some way twists the words of every one of the four speakers, including himself. Hermocrates's (20 C, 26 A); Socrates's (26 D); Timaeus's (27 C-29 D, 106 B-107 B); his own ("παραχρῆμα," 26 A, 107 E).

[2] See Ch. I, n. 4.

facts that it was in the Mediterranean instead of the Atlantic, that it flourished at least 6,500 years too late, and that its candidacy for the dishonor of being Atlantis rests largely on its presumed destruction by cataclysm, whereas Critias's story is preeminently concerned with the character of, and war between, the two cities, and hardly at all with their ultimate destruction. The fit is made even more tenuous by the legitimate suspicion that the simultaneous cataclysms which finally destroy both societies in Plato's story are simply a device for ending a tall tale and isolating it from recognizable historical experience—much as the statements that Athens came into existence 9,000 years earlier and that, after many generations, the war between the two cities took place 9,000 years earlier, provide a fanciful chronology (23 E, 112 C-D, 108 E).

Furthermore, the candidacy of Thera suffers from the same weakness as every other candidacy based solely on geographic or geological considerations: it is completely silent regarding what is surely the main point of Critias's story, its moral implications. Essentially the story is about a good city and a city gone bad and the divinely arranged, therapeutic punishment of the bad city by its defeat at the hands of the good. It claims the authority of Solon, the great moralist of Athenian political history:

> The citizens themselves, intent on only wealth,
> Wish in their folly to destroy the great city,
> They and their unjust chiefs who soon will pay
> The heavy price of their exceeding hybris.[3]

It comes from the hand of Plato, the moralist par excellence who begins this work with Socrates's desire to see good men in action, who ends Timaeus's monologue with a description of the reward awaiting the good and the therapeutic punishment awaiting the wicked, and who organized the whole work as a drama of the good man's victory and the bad man's defeat. And so it is hard to see how any alleged fit to the story can be of much consequence if it is merely geographical and has nothing to say about the moral considerations which were Plato's chief concern.

The requirement that the fit should be moral suggests a way out of the dilemma in which we are left by our conviction that the

---

[3] West, II, 121.

story is in some sense true and our knowledge that it does not describe any known history. In the long argument between the literalists and fictionalists a third possibility has been overlooked, that of parable. A parable is a story of events ostensibly remote from the time and/or place of the teller which in reality describes events very close and important to him and interprets them morally. In order to understand what the author considers to be the truth of the parable, we have to identify the events which it is really describing and interpreting. In the case of Critias's story the object of the search is clearly defined: we must look for a war between a small, modest and virtuous land power, and a large, rich and arrogant maritime power. Among events close and important to Plato two such wars preeminently stand forth, the Persian and the Peloponnesian.

In the first of these Persia was the wealthy, maritime, insolent and attacking power. Under Cyrus and Darius she had managed to keep control of herself in spite of her constantly increasing wealth and power. But with Xerxes, as at last with the rulers of Atlantis, the force of tradition and piety weakened. Forgetting his father's advice, Xerxes grew arrogant and expanded his fleet for an attack on Hellas. The host set out, like Atlantis, to enslave the Greeks, and the gods contrived their destruction, as they had contrived Atlantis's, mainly at the hands of little Athens. In both cases the insolent followers of Poseidon, no longer able to support the burden of their wealth and power, were struck down by the Greek city-states with Athena's little city of farmers and artisans at their head. The sequence of wealth, perfunctory recitation of traditional precepts, maritime power, and hybris led to disaster at the hands of a small but virtuous land power.

But in the half century after Salamis the parts of Solon's good and bad belligerents came to be acted by different states. Athenian wealth and power quickly multiplied, and two generations grew up and came to power who, like Critias, enjoyed the fad of declaiming Solon's ethical poetry and the luxury of missing its point. The little land power became a great sea power. Instead of liberating the islands after repelling their conquerors, as the little Athens of Solon's story had done, this Athens kept them, in the manner of Persia and Atlantis. As Plato says elsewhere, "Though education brings victory, victory sometimes defeats education. For men have often grown insolent after defeating their enemies, and

through their insolence they have been led into countless other
vices, ... and many a victory has been and will be disastrous to
the victors" (*Laws*, 641).[4] When on the Panathenaea the Athenian
orators commemorated their brave forefathers' rout of the insolent
Persians, they failed to see that in describing the greed and arro-
gance of the Persians they were really describing themselves and
that they were rushing on the same doom in the same way for the
same reasons.[5] The victors over the insolent Persians went the way
of Persia until Pericles, instead of enslaving only the Hellespont
like Xerxes, could tell his bemused listeners, "I declare to you
that of the two elements accessible to man, the land and the sea,
you are the absolute masters of one, rule as much of it as you wish,
and can rule as much more as you choose." [6] By this time, though
neither realized it, Critias was an Atlantid through and through
and Athens a full-blown Atlantis, and their patron deity was no
longer Athena but Poseidon.[7]

As Athens grew into the part of Atlantis, the role of the small
and virtuous land power which she had deserted was filled by
Sparta. Thus was the Persian war repeated in the Peloponnesian:
once more the small, ascetic, land-fighting power defeated the
wealthy, maritime, insolent and aggressive empire. Hence both
wars could be truly represented by one war between two cities of
these antithetical natures. This fusing of the two wars into one
is the reason why each of Critias's two belligerent powers itself
exhibits the local characteristics of two similar societies. His
ancient Athens is a compound of Athenian geography and sixth
century Athenian simplicity and Spartan institutions. His Atlantis
is a luxuriant pastiche of Asian flora and fauna, of Persian and
late fifth century Athenian wealth and seafaring and ostentation,
and of Persian and Athenian hybris. Like Asia it has elephants

---

[4] At *Laws* 704 A-707 C Plato deplores in general the imitation by a
state of the bad habits of its enemies, in particular the imitation by a coastal
state of the vicious practice of seafaring, and most particularly the imitation
by Athens of Persian naval warfare. Note the implication in this passage
that when Athens did not imitate Minos and become a sea power, she
remained sound, but when she did imitate Persia, it was the beginning of her
downfall.

[5] Proclus, I. 172.

[6] Thuc. II. 62. 2.

[7] Forman, in the introduction to his edition of Aristophanes *Nub.*, p. 18,
castigates the greed and insolence of Athens and Pericles in language strikingly similar to the castigation of Atlantis at the end of the *T-C*.

and a vast pharmacopoeia and hot and cold running water. Like Xerxes's Persia and Pericles's Athens it commands the sea. Shorey's ear, though alert, was not overly impressionable when he heard the bustle of the Piraeus in the never-ending noise and confusion of the port of Atlantis, and Aristophanes's theology was sound when he recognized Poseidon, who was to be the god of Plato's Atlantis, as the god of late fifth-century Athens, too. But perhaps Pericles should have the honor of the surest identification of Athens with Atlantis, for it was he who told his fellow citizens to think of their city as an impregnable island.[8]

And so when we are told at the end of Critias's story that the defeat of Atlantis was the punishment of her hybris arranged by the gods, we learn Plato's view of the cause and purpose of both wars on which he looked back. Early fifth century Athens led the Greeks in carrying out the divine sentence on Persian hybris. Late fifth century Sparta led her allies in carrying out the divine sentence on Periclean Athens, drunk with greed and insolence. Both wars were the execution of the same divine judgement on the same type of malefactor through the agency of the same type of benefactor, and their moral aspect could be represented with consummate accuracy by an account of one war.

We can consider the story true, then, in two senses. Seeing that this one story accurately describes the moral and theological aspects of both the great wars in Greek history, we can well suppose that it should explain many other wars as well, that, like Plato's ideas, it reveals a paradigmatic and universal truth. This is the model account, the true explanation, of the fate of nations as their nature and training generate policies and institutions and as they meet one another in war throughout history. It is this moral or universal truth which the Egyptian priest and Solon in their superior wisdom tried to convey to their listeners. By Critias's time the story proves to be also locally and particularly true, for it is the history of fifth-century Athens and Greece. Though, as Solon said and Critias perfunctorily repeats, such things are not perceived by "those who are unable to see what is the truly happy

---

[8] *Il.* xxii, 147-52; Shorey, 351; Aristoph. *Eq.* 562 ff.; Thuc. I. 143 (cf. Gomme, I, 461). Many others have noticed these and other parallels between Atlantis and Persia or Athens; none, so far as I know, has suggested this purpose of Plato's in reflecting both in the same mirror.

life" (121 B), this is the true history of Critias's own time and place.[9]

We can now see the full irony of Critias's falling silent just as he describes the punishment of Atlantis—he is himself a true Atlantid; the wicked city and its wicked citizen are struck down together. And if Critias's disappearance is the punishment not only of a wicked man but of a typical Athenian, we can now make a more informed guess as to the identity of the suddenly stricken and therefore missing fourth partner, who, disappearing sooner than Critias, was perhaps even more wicked than Critias.[10] Is it not extremely likely that he was that arch-Atlantid, Pericles, who in 429 fell fatally ill of the plague around the season of the Panathenaea?[11] In this case nothing could be more natural or serious than what looks like Timaeus's somewhat forced humor at the beginning, ". . .those of us who are left. . .," and his long discussion of diseases (81 E-87 B) could hardly be more timely. The Zeus-sent illness of Pericles, moreover, could hardly be richer in irony, for he had so bemused the Athenians by his majestic presence and omniscient oratory that they had conferred on him the title of Olympian Zeus.[12]

---

[9] The tragedy of Critias epitomizes that of Athens. Just as Critias admired Solon's fame but failed to perceive or heed the moral of his story, so the Athenians celebrated (particularly on the Panathenaea, cf. Proclus, I. 172) the glorious deeds of their forefathers in defeating the Persians, but failed to perceive or heed the moral of that defeat. For them the history of the Persian wars was an exciting and flattering story, just as Solon's tale was for Critias.

[10] For an indication at the very beginning of the work that the absentee is of the mold of Critias rather than Timaeus, see Ch. II, n. 9.

[11] For a summary of Plato's attitude to Pericles, see Welliver, 26-40. Pericles died in the autumn of 429 (Thuc. II. 65; Gomme, II, 190) and fell ill a considerable time before (Plut. V. Per. 38.1). For the Panathenaea see Ch. II, n. 10. If this conjecture as to the identity of the missing fourth partner is correct, the dramatic date of the T-C is 429, some three years after the Charmides, roughly the same as the Gorgias and Protagoras, some five years before the Republic (Taylor Comm, 15 f.; see p. 54 below). If Critias is ninety years old (as his grandfather was when he told the story), he would have been born in 519, his grandfather in 599, his great-grandfather, Dropides, in 640-30. Solon was born between 640 and 625 (Davies, 323-4; cf. p. 51 below).

[12] Aristoph. Acharn. 530. The following paragraph (Welliver, 60) suggests some of the irony in 17 A-B, if it refers to Pericles.

> That the hero of heroes should cut such a sorry figure! That he who was always haranguing his audience about their duties as heirs and "survivors" should have to leave to survivors the performance of his duty—and, worse yet, to a non-Athenian survivor who mockingly uses

The last and utmost irony is reserved, as it should be, for Socrates. For while the false imitator of Zeus was struck down by Zeus at the outset, Socrates is revealed at the end as the truly Zeus-like man. Just as Zeus lured Atlantis to its fatal attack on little Athens in order that it might strike a truer note, so does the suspicion of luring Critias and the others to attack Timaeus inevitably fall on Socrates. He it is, after all, who precipitates the action by speaking the day before and asking his listeners to speak for him in return. He it is who turns to Critias and Hermocrates and first addresses them by name only as he is about to flatter them with the suggestion that they are philosophers and statesmen (19 A). And he it is who urges Critias to tell his story and applauds his program of talks (26 E, 27 B). Surely he knew how true Atlantids would behave toward a good partner in such a situation and what the penalty for such behavior was likely to be. Beside the childish plot of the three Atlantids to get the better of Timaeus, Socrates's plot to bring them back into tune with the cosmos is the providence of God.

---

his imperial catchwords to speak of justice! In his funeral speech Pericles had observed, by way of contrast with Athens' spontaneous generosity, that one who already owes another a good turn, knows that his help will not be interpreted as good will but only as the repayment of a debt, and is therefore not quick to offer it. That such a one, owing Socrates a good turn, should have been harshly prevented from paying his debt, and that he should be described as sorry only to have been prevented from joining the discussion! That the paragon of foresight and manliness, who accused his opponents of being sick in their judgement, should have been prevented from coming by an unforeseen illness! That the arch votary of Poseidon should be stricken on the festival of Athena!

CHAPTER SEVEN

PLATONIC TRAGEDY

We have now followed the delineation of character and the unfolding of plot through the work and have touched on the element of thought in interpreting Critias's story. It remains to say something of the thought of the work as a whole and to appraise it anew as art and drama in the light of the foregoing discussion.

The arbitrary category of thought comprises primarily Timaeus's discourse and Critias's story abstracted from the character of the speakers and the events of the drama in which they are embedded. This is, in fact, the aspect of the work which has almost exclusively attracted the attention of readers, and the apparent incongruity between the two components of the thought has certainly been responsible, along with the apparent incompleteness of the work, for discouraging suspicion that it may be a finished work of art, and perhaps for its division in antiquity into two separate parts.[1] Critias's story seems strangely yoked with Timaeus's account of the origins of the cosmos and mankind, and his pretension that Timaeus's account should be but a prelude to his story seems preposterous.

We should remember, however, that the author of the thought which Critias recites is, according to Plato, not Critias but Solon. Critias is a pitiful figure of drama, a man sick with hybris who tells a story of which the moral is that hybris is fatal. But *qua* thought the story is represented as Solon's, though of course he is in part indebted to Egyptian wisdom for his inspiration, just as Timaeus is indebted to preceding cosmologists (29 E). When we consider the thought separately, abstracted from the character and plot of the drama, we should convert the *dramatis personae* to a *philosophiae personae*: we should think of Solon as the real partner of Timaeus.[2] Socrates's praise of the speakers as philosophers and statesmen would then ring true.[3]

---

[1] See Appendix B.

[2] Like Timaeus and Socrates, Solon and Socrates are closely attuned: Critias says (25 E), "ἐθαύμαζον... κατανοῶν ὡς δαιμονίως ἔκ τινος τύχης οὐκ ἄπο σκοποῦ ξυνηνέχθης τὰ πολλὰ οἷς Σόλων εἶπεν."

[3] 120 E-121 C could have come straight from Solon. Compare Solon's

In spite of the appearance of incongruity in the juxtaposition of the two stories, they are in fact complementary. Timaeus's demiurge, in whom no envy ever arises, creates the subordinate gods as far as possible in his own image (29 E, 41 A-D); Solon's Zeus is friendly (φιλόφρων) and gentle (πρᾶος), his pantheon is just and not grasping (120 E, 109 B). The demiurge delegates to the subordinate gods the creation and governance of men, and Timaeus sets forth the principles of this creation and governance (41 A-D). Solon's Athena and Hephaestus and Poseidon set particular men in particular times and places, and Zeus intervenes in a particular crisis (109 B, 113 C, 120-21). Where Timaeus announces the laws of destiny to which all men are subject and the penalty for their violation (41 E-42 B), Solon shows some men in the act of obeying and violating them and Zeus punishing the violation. The story of the two cities is a local parable illustrating the universal principles which Timaeus sets forth. Solon adds the concrete to the abstract, process to genesis, judgement to legislation, the historical fate of nations to the decreed fate of individuals. A historical figure, he translates the divine purpose into laws of history, as Timaeus, an unhistorical figure, translates it into the laws of the cosmos and of man's destiny.

If we believe that the inspiration of the parable which Plato so appropriately attributes to Solon was the course of fifth century Athenian history, then it supplements Timaeus's discourse in another and more striking way: it demonstrates the inference of divine purpose from historical phenomena, just as Timaeus demonstrates the inference of divine purpose from physical phenomena. Plato looks at the design of the universe and of man and sees that these imply a goodness and harmony in all things which it is the will of man's creator that he should imitate. Conversely he looks at the character and fate of historical cities and sees that these imply the execution of divine punishment on societies which have fallen hopelessly out of tune with the manifest laws of the cosmos. The divine nature and purpose are at the heart of both Plato's philosophy of history, enunciated by Solon, and his philosophy of nature and man, enunciated by Timaeus.

---

pleasure in hearing more, in spite of the fact that his instructors have called him an ignoramus (22 A-23 D), with Timaeus's willingness to be proved wrong (54 A).

Like a refrain the phrase or idea "deeds and words" (ἔργα καὶ λόγοι) recurs in Socrates's proemial speech (19 B-20 C). The citizens whom he has described he would like to see in action. He would like to see the fruits of their education "in their performance of deeds and in their verbal negotiations during the fighting" (ἐν τῷ πολεμεῖν κατά τε τὰς ἐν τοῖς ἔργοις πράξεις καὶ κατὰ τὰς ἐν τοῖς λόγοις διερμηνεύσεις). It is hard for men to imitate in action what they do not know, and still harder in words. The Sophists will not understand how philosophers and statesmen would "act and speak" (πράττοντες ἔργῳ καὶ λόγῳ προσομιλοῦντες). Timaeus is distinguished in both the active and contemplative lives. Socrates spoke that he might be repaid with a demonstration of war. At the outset we are alerted to the continuous interpenetration of word and deed.

The locus in art of words and deeds intertwined is drama, and Plato's insistence on the combination of the two at the beginning of this work is consistent with our discovery in it of a finely designed drama. More than any other dialogue except the *Symposium* the *Timaeus-Critias* is a drama in the sense of the intricate articulation of speech and deeds. Alone among Plato's works it is a tragedy, his only surviving tragedy, one might say, remembering the tradition that he wrote tragedies in his youth and later destroyed them.[4] Long after the fact it furnishes the proof of the contention which Socrates forces on his drowsy comrades at the end of the *Symposium*: "Socrates was forcing them to agree that the same man could write comedy and tragedy." To the uniquely Platonic comedy of the *Symposium* the *Timaeus-Critias* furnishes the pendant of a uniquely Platonic tragedy.[5] Half an orbit removed from marking the nadir of Plato's creative abilities, the work shows them in many ways at their zenith, discovering an unprecedented way of integrating thought and character and action, crowning the long series of more episodic sketches or more circumscribed subjects with a universal design.

As tragedy the *Timaeus-Critias* undoubtedly has both a polemic and a positive mission. Plato's outspoken criticism of tragedy in the *Republic* and his subtler attack on the poets here, justify us in

---

[4] Diog. Laert. III. 5.

[5] Including, however, the high comedy of Socrates and Timaeus. "Si grand que soit l'artifice du rheteur ou du sophiste, la vérité a des armes invincibles, qui doivent à la fin triompher;" Rivaud *PAD*, 140.

looking for an anti-poetic element in his own tragedy, and it is not hard to find. His chief accusation against the poets is that they seduce our reason from its duty of controlling the emotions.

> You know that the very best of us, when we hear Homer or some other of the makers of tragedy imitating one of the heroes who is in grief and is delivering a long tirade in his lamentations or chanting and beating his breast, feel pleasure and abandon ourselves and accompany the representation with sympathy and eagerness, and we praise as an excellent poet the one who most strongly affects us in this way. . . But when in our own lives some affliction comes to us, you are also aware that we plume ourselves upon the opposite, on our ability to remain calm and endure, in the belief that this is the conduct of a man and what we were praising in the theater that of a woman (*Rep.* 605 C-E).

What more appropriate challenge could there be to this bombastic tragedy than a work which at first sight does not even appear to be a tragedy? And what better antidote to tragedy in which emotion overcomes the reason than a tragedy where reason is supreme, where indeed emotion seems hardly to enter until the reader has penetrated far beneath the surface with his reason? What the *Timaeus-Critias* asks of the spectator is to exercise his utmost powers of thought both to follow the thought of the work and to detect the very strong feelings which lie concealed beneath its deceptively expository surface. It is a masterful attack on a tragedy which, according to Plato, drowned thought in emotion.

But Plato as the Platonic poet is more interesting than Plato the anti-poet. The more important aspect of the work as drama is its illustration in its very design and unfolding of his fundamental faith in the explanation of phenomena by purpose. Circling back on itself, answering the questions which it excites, seeming to end in accident but proving to end by design, intimating purpose in every detail, even as the heavenly bodies and the bodies of men reveal their maker's purposes in their every detail, it is Plato's portrayal and representation of the cosmos: "One world alone, a round body turning around, solitary. . . , enabled by its excellence to be itself company for itself and needing none besides, sufficient acquaintance and friend to itself" (κύκλῳ δὴ κύκλον στρεφόμενον οὐρανὸν ἕνα μόνον ἔρημον . . . , δι' ἀρετὴν δὲ αὐτὸν αὑτῷ δυνάμενον ξυγγίγνεσθαι καὶ οὐδενὸς ἑτέρου προσδεόμενον, γνώριμον δὲ καὶ φίλον ἱκανῶς αὐτὸν αὑτῷ; 34 B).

4

WHICH CRITIAS?

After more than half a century of uncertainty there is still no agreement as to whether we should take the Critias in Plato's *Timaeus* and *Critias* to be "the tyrant" or his grandfather. The task of identifying him must begin with the two passages from his opening remarks to Socrates in the introduction to the *Timaeus* (20 E-21 B).

> Now [Solon] was a relative and very close friend of my great-grandfather, Dropides, as he himself often says in his poems; and he told my grandfather, Critias, as the old man in turn used to repeat to us, that great and marvellous were the exploits of this city in ancient times. . .
> I will tell you an old story from a man not young. For indeed at that time Critias, as he said, was very nearly ninety years old, while I was somewhere about ten.

Throughout antiquity and until the beginning of this century the speaker of these words was assumed to be the Critias who lived from about 460 to 403, was a member of the Thirty, was denominated "the tyrant" or "the oligarch," and was a first cousin once removed of Plato.[1]

When Kirchner, in preparing his *Prosopographia Attica* in the last years of the nineteenth century, faced the chronological realities of the situation, he realized that it was impossible for the grandfather of the tyrant, who could hardly have been born before about 540, to have spoken with Solon (c. 630-c. 558). He therefore concluded that the stemma by which the tyrant descended from Dropides must have contained two more generations than were recognized in antiquity; but he continued to identify the Critias of the *Timaeus* and *Critias* with the tyrant, in spite of the apparent corollary of this identification that Plato had erred by two generations in tracing his family back to the time of Solon.[2] In 1914

---

[1] Diog. Laert., III. 1; Greene, 280.

[2] Kirchner, s. vv. Dropides, Kritias, Platon, and stemma for Plato. Diogenes Laertius had added a generation to the interval between Dropides and Plato by making Callaischros Plato's great-grandfather instead of his great-uncle; but this had no effect on the interval between Dropides and the tyrant.

Burnet proposed what seemed a self-evident solution of this
anomaly: the Critias who speaks in the dialogues is not the tyrant
but rather his grandfather, who was also Plato's great-grandfather.[3] An ostrakon found near the Athenian agora in 1936,
published in 1949, and first related to Plato's genealogy by Davies
in his *Athenian Propertied Families* (1971), provided additional
and better evidence of the existence of this elder Critias and the
first evidence for his father, Leaides.[4] Thus Davies was able to
cite evidence for every generation in the stemma from Dropides to
Plato, an abstract from which follows (the Roman numerals
distinguishing homonyms are Davies's; the approximate dates of
birth in the sixth century differ slightly from Davies's).

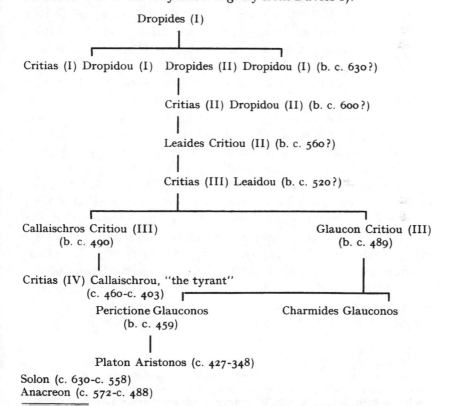

Solon (c. 630-c. 558)
Anacreon (c. 572-c. 488)

---

[3] Burnet *GP*, 338, note. Cf. Burnet *EGP*, 203, n. 3. Burnet also attributed
to the elder Critias that part of the works of "Critias" previously attributed
to the tyrant. This is not necessary for the identification of Plato's Critias as
the elder Critias. Burnet was probably induced to make the attribution by
what he considered Socrates's compliment to Critias at 20 B; but see pp. 10 f.
[4] *Hesperia*, Supp. 8, 1949, 359, no. 12; Davies, 325-6. The only previously
known evidence of the existence of this Critias was the scholion on Aesch.
Prom. 128 (see p. 54).

4*

In 1949 Rosenmeyer vigorously attacked Burnet's thesis and proposed a return to the identification of Plato's raconteur as Critias the tyrant and to the corollary of Plato's ignorance of his own genealogy.[5] Davies, in a brief discussion of the problem included in his account of Plato's and the tyrant's genealogy, agreed with the Kirchner-Rosenmeyer identification and tried to relieve their solution of the burden of asserting Plato's ignorance by offering a theory of his intentional misrepresentation of his genealogy.[6] To judge from the lack of any published dissent from Rosenmeyer's and Davies's conclusions, they seem for the moment to have won the day, but the arguments on which they rest are so questionable that their authority must be considered precarious in the extreme.[7]

Critias's age. If Plato's Critias is a very old man, as Burnet maintained, he cannot be the tyrant, who died in his late fifties. Rosenmeyer rightly objected, however, that Plato nowhere calls him a very old man.[8] But against this objection it can be urged that Critias says that Solon's poems were a novelty in his youth (21 B), a statement which, though it is hard to see how it could be literally true of a time fifty years after Solon's death, is yet less arrestingly false the older we suppose Critias to be (and, of course, the earlier we suppose the dialogues to have taken place).[9] Furthermore, Critias speaks of the story told him by his grandfather as "ταῦτα ἃ πάμπολυν χρόνον διακήκοα" (26 B).[10] In addition to these passages Burnet (and Taylor and Cornford) may well have been influenced by less explicit considerations: the tendency of the very old to recall vividly scenes from their childhood; the reader's feeling that, since Critias is repeating the narrative triumph of his grandfather, he is of a like age; the pervading theme of the very old passing the story down to the young—the εὖ μάλα παλαιός priest of ancient Egypt (22 B) told the story to Solon, the child-like Greek; Solon told it to Critias II, perhaps some thirty years

---

[5] Rosenmeyer *FC*.

[6] Davies, 325-6.

[7] Rivaud, *TC* (17), Guthrie (298), Luce (23), believe Critias to be the tyrant; Levinson (359) is uncertain. Prof. Luce, to judge from the opinion which he expressed in a public lecture after reading this essay, appears to have changed his mind.

[8] Rosenmeyer *FC*, 406.

[9] See pp. 44 and 54.

[10] Rosenmeyer, who elsewhere follows Bury's translation (404, note 4), here softens Bury's rendering of "πάμπολυν χρόνον" from "such a great time ago" to "quite some time ago" (*FC*, 406).

his junior; Critias II told it when he was ninety to his ten-year-old grandson.

Rosenmeyer further argued that, since Plato's Critias refers to his grandfather as an old man (παλαιός, πρεσβύτης), Critias cannot himself be an old man.[11] In the absence of any justification of this inference I assume that it resulted from a feeling that it would be unnatural for an old, but natural for a middle-aged, man to refer to his grandfather as an old man. But the grandson's first references to his grandfather as old (γέρων) are in a context which makes them perfectly natural regardless of the grandson's present age: he is emphasizing the great age of the story and its narrator ("Ἐγὼ φράσω παλαιὸν ἀκηκοὼς λόγον οὐ νέου ἀνδρός") and he shows the narrator telling the story on Children's Day not just to him but to many children and other members of the φρατρία, for whom he was impressively γέρων (20 D-21 D). When later the grandson again recalls his grandfather's telling the story (which is the passage cited by Rosenmeyer as evidence that the grandson is not old), references to the grandfather as old have no more bearing on the grandson's present age than did the earlier references, for he is still reliving the scene of the old man and his audience on that far-off Children's Day. Besides, those of us who have reached a certain age are apt to be quite unconscious of any incongruity, if indeed there is any, in our referring to others as old.

Critias, the tyrant, in the Charmides. Rosenmeyer says that in the *Charmides* (157 E) "two of the oligarch's ancestors, Dropides and Critias, are quoted by name for their friendship with famous men of letters. In the *Timaeus*, Critias similarly cites the names of his ancestors, Dropides and Critias, and extols their literary connections. The conclusion is self-evident: the Critias of the *Timaeus* is identical with the Critias of the *Charmides*, i.e. he is the oligarch." [12] The conclusion is not at all self-evident. Dropides and Critias were, after all, ancestors of both Critias III and Critias, the tyrant, and there is no reason whatever why the intimacy of the family with illustrious poets should not be mentioned in connection with both of these descendants. Indeed comparable situations in my own experience suggest that a family's intimacy with illustrious men is inevitably mentioned by *all* of its descendants.

---

[11] Rosenmeyer *FC*, 406; *T-C* 25 D, 26 B; cf. 20 E, 21 C.
[12] Rosenmeyer *FC*, 408.

Critias and Anacreon. Rosenmeyer argued from a scholion on Aeschylus *Prom.* 128, according to which Critias was loved by the poet, Anacreon, and from the tradition of Anacreon's birth in 572, that Critias III could not have been born after 540.[13] If this were true, he could hardly have participated in the colloquium of the *Timaeus*, which, on the assumption that Socrates (b. 469) was by then at least thirty-five years old, must have taken place no earlier than 434. But if we add the margin of error of at least ten years in the date of Anacreon's birth to the less easily determined but surely no smaller margin in our estimate of the decline of his libido, we must admit that Rosenmeyer's latest possible date of Critias's birth could well be in error by twenty years.[14] On this reckoning the colloquium of the *Timaeus* could have taken place as late as 430 before Critias's age would have exceeded ninety.

The dramatic date of the Timaeus and Critias. The dramatic date of the dialogues is, of course, important for the decision as to whether Plato's Critias is the tyrant or his grandfather—the later the date, the more likely the tyrant; the earlier, the more likely the grandfather. The presence in Athens of the Syracusan general, Hermocrates, the fourth participant in the dialogues, argues an early date: Athens first went to war with Syracuse in 427, and Hermocrates was accusing her of designs on Sicily at least as early as 424 and would presumably have been *persona non grata* in Athens by then, if not sooner.[15] Rosenmeyer simply discarded this consideration ("much too problematical to help us").[16] On the other hand he was glad to follow Cornford and others in dissociating the dramatic date of the *Timaeus* from that of the *Republic*, which Taylor fixed at about 424, because this leaves us free to date the *Timaeus* and *Critias* "at any time in the late fifth century prior to the. . . . death of Hermocrates" (408).[17] But it leaves us equally free, it should be noted, to date the dialogues at any time *prior* to 424 which other considerations may urge.

---

[13] Rosenmeyer *FC*, 407.

[14] The evidence (in 'Suidas') for the date of Anacreon's birth is hopelessly corrupt (Rohde, 190; cf. Bowra, 269). Even the assumption that he was a grown man at the time of the Teans' migration to Abdera ca. 541, based on presumed allusions to Teos in some of his poems, is questionable (Bowra, 270). On this assumption he could have been born as late as 562 and would have been about fifty-seven years old when Critias III was about fifteen.

[15] Thuc. III. 86; IV. 58-65.

[16] Rosenmeyer *FC*, 409.

[17] *Ibid.*; Taylor *Comm*, 14-16.

Plato's accuracy. Confessing at once that this is a prejudice of long standing, I am skeptical of Rosenmeyer's thesis because of its dependence on a kind of explanation which I call the imbecillic theory of genius. "Plato himself, writing two hundred years after Solon and more than two generations after Critias [the oligarch], neglected to inquire into the exact number of generations intervening between Solon and the oligarch." [18] Can we really believe that the man whose powers of inquiry have been the admiration of all posterity and who shows us Solon counting the generations and calculating the years back to Deucalion (22 A-B), did not accurately count the generations and years back to Solon?

Intentional anachronism. Davies apparently also found the above argument implausible and undertook to relieve the Kirchner-Rosenmeyer solution of its burden by advancing the theory that Plato intentionally abbreviated his own genealogy.[19] Taking it for granted that Plato's raconteur is the tyrant, Davies argued, in effect, as follows:

1) Critias's remark about the newness of Solon's poems in his youth makes Critias seem closer to Solon than he really was;
2) Plato committed this anachronism in order to make the transmission of the story through so long a period seem more plausible; [20]

---

[18] Rosenmeyer *FC*, 408. This is a somewhat misleading statement of the matter. Plato wrote the *Timaeus-Critias* late in life (Taylor *Comm*, 3-13); more important than when he wrote it is when he might reasonably be assumed to have learned about his ancestors. When he was sixteen (c. 411), his grandfather and great-uncle would have been about seventy-eight years old. If either of them was still living, he could have learned his genealogy at least as far back as the father of Critias III, for they surely knew who their grandfather was. This would have been far enough back to allow the conclusion that this man was the son of the Critias, son of Dropides, mentioned in a poem of Solon's (West, II, 133). The mention of a Callaischros by Lysias (XII. 66) has been taken to prove that the great-uncle was still living in 411, but see Davies, 327-8. It should also be remembered that it is the almost universal practice of aristocratic families to keep accurate genealogical records.
[19] Davies, 325-6.
[20] In one respect Davies's argument here seems somewhat misleading: it gives the impression that this guess as to Plato's purpose is supported by other purposes which the anachronistic remark might well have served, i.e. that Plato needed a "bridge passage" to introduce Solon or that he wanted to locate the Apatouria in the remote past. But no anachronism would have been required for the effecting of these other purposes: Solon's poems need

3) the omission of two generations from Plato's genealogy, i.e. his use of the tyrant as his raconteur, would have the same effect as (1);

4) therefore we can assume that Plato committed also this anachronism for the same reason for which he committed (1).

Now this argument really has little bearing on the question, which Critias is Plato's raconteur, for it is not an argument that the tyrant is the raconteur but rather that, if he is, then this would explain Plato's motive for using him. As against arguments that the text and the historical facts do not require us to believe that Plato committed the anachronism of using him, however, the argument that we can find a reason why he might have committed it is not very cogent.

Nor is the reason itself persuasive. To show an actor lying, as even the older Critias would be lying in asserting the novelty of Solon's poems in his youth, is one thing, but to erase the memory of two generations of the author's own family in the interests of plausibility is quite another.[21] It smacks of impiety and of the Sophists.[22] We should not so lightly believe that Plato would deny the existence of two generations of his own ancestors and trifle with the truth for the sake of a little plausibility.[23]

Nor is Davies's guess as to Plato's motive in making Critias commit his anachronism convincing. It seems hardly likely that Plato would be much concerned about the plausibility of the transmission through some one hundred and forty years of a story recounting events 9,000 years in the past, which took place at

---

not have been new to be recited, and the Apatouria is obviously very remote if the grandson of the man to whom Solon told his story was then only ten years old.

[21] Of course Critias's purpose in committing his anachronism, as distinct from Plato's in having him commit it, may well be that of enhancing the plausibility of his account; see Ch. II, n. 15.

[22] It might be objected that to show the author's great-grandfather lying also smacks of impiety. But, to adapt the argument of *Gorg.* 480 B-D, if he really was a liar (and worse), it would be a favor to him to say so and to show his punishment.

[23] Furthermore, Davies's whole argument risks falling of its own weight by asserting that Plato is trying to make the transmission of his story more plausible by accumulating implausibilities (the text itself exposes the first anachronism: it is obviously most implausible that the poems of Solon could still have been new by the time his contemporary's great-grandson was ten years old). Nothing detracts from plausibility like lying.

least 1,000 years before the account of them was recorded (23 E).
What we have seen of Critias's character makes it seem far likelier
that Plato had him lie because he *is* a liar—that this anachronism
stamps him as a liar from the beginning and launches him on his
demonstration of lying and deceit. Describing the Feast of Ἀπάτη,
recalling the clansmen like Amynander who now and then and
particularly during the Apatouria lied, setting out to ensnare
Timaeus, Critias, like any other athlete, flexes his muscles and
tries his stride with an easy lie. The anachronism is his, not Plato's.[24]

The great strength of the Burnet solution is that it and it alone
agrees with what we know of the facts of Plato's genealogy. Davies
contributed to this strength by his painstaking confirmation of
that genealogy, which at a more tentative stage led Burnet to
propose his solution, and particularly by calling attention to the
evidence that a candidate for ostracism named Critias was living
in Athens in the early fifth century, when the tyrant's grandfather
would have been in middle age. I find no serious objection to
believing that it is he whom we should see and hear telling Solon's
story around 430, when he is about ninety years old.

---

[24] See Ch. II, n. 15.

APPENDIX B

DID PLATO WRITE THE *CRITIAS* AS A SEPARATE WORK?

The history of the text does not extend far enough back to throw any light on the question of whether Plato wrote the *Timaeus-Critias* as one continuous work or as two.[1] The frequent assertion that the *Critias* was published posthumously is only conjecture, inspired by its apparently fragmentary state. Its status as a separate work in the earliest canons does entail, to be sure, a presumption of separate composition, but on the other hand there are several indications that the two works were once one.

The most obvious argument for original continuity is the incongruity of the hiatus between the cessation of Timaeus's words at the end of the *Timaeus* and the conclusion of his monologue at the beginning of the *Critias*. It is very hard to read *Critias* 106 A-B without feeling that somehow this eloquent prayer, so consonant with all that has gone before and with what immediately precedes it ("δίκην," cf. 92 B; "θεῷ γεγονότι," cf. 92 C), so expressive of Timaeus's character, so summary of his spirit of inquiry, has been torn from its proper place. It is clearly symmetrical with his exordium: he addresses Socrates here as he addressed him there; as he began with a prayer that God would approve what he was about to say, he ends with a prayer that God has approved what he has said; and as he acknowledged at the beginning that some of his discourse would doubtless be inaccurate, he acknowledges the same thing at the end (27 C-29 D). All of these sentiments are not only suitable but, as expressions of courtesy, friendship, and piety, indispensable, to a proper ending. The prayer is the unmistakeable conclusion of the monologue and seems to beg the pious reader, with the eloquence of an Elpenor or a Palinurus, to remove the barrier that separates it from the noble discourse which it should crown.

Some measure of the unnaturalness of the division is afforded by two problems of interpretation which it poses. Timaeus prays to "τῷ... πρὶν μὲν πάλαι ποτ᾽ ἔργῳ, νῦν δὲ λόγοις ἄρτι θεῷ γεγονότι"

---

[1] See Alline, 17-34; Philip, 301, 305 ff.

(106 A), a continuation of the language he has just used in *Timaeus* 92 C. This means "to the god who. . . has *just now* come into being in words" and implies that Timaeus has just this minute finished describing him; but Bury, apparently troubled by that implication, translates "who has recently been created by our speech" (for the sense of "νῦν. . . ἄρτι" in Plato see *Polit.* 291 A, B; Rivaud translates "á l'instant"). The problem would disappear if there were no division, and hence no implied passage of time, between the *Timaeus* and the *Critias*.

At 110D Critias says that the ancient Athenians "engaged in those activities which were mentioned yesterday in the description of the proposed guardians." The natural assumption is that this refers to Socrates's discourse of the previous day, but some interpreters, presumably wishing an interval between the *Timaeus* and *Critias* more proportionate to their separation, have read "χθές" as a reference to Socrates's recapitulation of that discourse in the *Timaeus* and therefore as dating the *Critias* on the day after the *Timaeus*.[2] This chronology clashes, however, with the clear evidence for the delivery of both monologues on the same day: it is twice observed (21 A, 26 E) that Critias's story will be appropriate to the Panathenaea, the second remark referring unequivocally to Critias's second telling of the story; the first remark implies, and the second proves, that they are made on the day of the Panathenaea; obviously Timaeus speaks on this same day; hence Critias delivers his monologue on the same day as does Timaeus.

The present study offers other arguments for continuity. If the *Timaeus-Critias* can be seen as a complete and unified composition, if the *Critias* is not an abandoned fragment, then it is much more likely that Plato wrote the whole as one work. In particular the denouement of the theme of the ὁμολογία at 106 B, the very close and careful articulation of Critias's exordium with the exordia of Socrates and Timaeus, and the light which the conversation at 108 A-D sheds on the enigmas which precede it, go far to support this conclusion.[3]

The most likely motive of Plato's successors for dividing what they may have found undivided would have been their belief that the two parts were of very unequal value. Timaeus's monologue must have seemed to them, as it has to later ages, a unique monu-

---

[2] E.g. Taylor *TC*, 112; cf. Bruns, 273.
[3] See Chaps. II-IV above.

ment to Plato's thought and knowledge, a powerful compendium
of his most sacred doctrines, and consequently the one work best
calculated to attract students and support. Should they send forth
so finished and elevated a work concluded and burdened by a
seeming fragment which would surely strike the kind of reader
for whom they intended the *Timaeus* as a piece of frivolous fiction—especially as the tale had already been completely and more
succinctly told at the beginning of the work? How could Critias's
unsuccessful effort to tell his story a second time do anything but
detract from the majesty of the magnum opus? It was pure anti-
climax, and so, I suspect, they decided to amputate it and were
forced to trim away Timaeus's closing words with it because in
these he transferred the burden of speaking to Critias.[4]

Where should they make the cut? There were two possibilities
only, the one they chose and a later one before "προσευξάμενοι
δέ" (106 B). The latter would have served very well, in some ways
better than the one they chose, had it not been for "προσευξάμενοι."
Unwilling either thus to mystify the reader of the *Critias* or to
corrupt Plato's text by omitting the troublesome participle, they
would have chosen the earlier alternative. This left the *Timaeus*
with a satisfactory, though somewhat prosaic, conclusion; and the
true conclusion of Timaeus' monologue had the virtue of setting
the stage for the *Critias* by its mention of Socrates, by its evidence
that Timaeus had "νῦν... ἄρτι" delivered the discourse which
Critias was about to emulate, and by its conferring of a certain
plausibility on Critias' deceitful insinuation that Timaeus had
spoken only about the gods.

---

[4] See Cherniss, Chap. III, for the state of the Academy after Plato, for
Plato's secretiveness (which would explain why his successors did not get
the point of the *T-C*), and for the character of Xenocrates (p. 82). See
Philip, 298, 301, 306, for the most likely circumstances of the editing and
publishing of the Platonic corpus, and Kirk, 594, for the intense competition
of Plato (and therefore of the Academy) with Sophistic education. Note
the agreement of this hypothesis with my contention (pp. 22, 32 f.) that
Plato *intended* Critias's monologue to seem anti-climactic as thought,
although of course his removal from the scene is the climax of the plot.

FRANCIS BACON'S UNDERSTANDING OF THE *TIMAEUS-CRITIAS*

It is possible that at least one earlier reader sensed the significance of the apparent incompleteness of the *Timaeus-Critias*. Francis Bacon wrote the *New Atlantis* with obvious reference to Plato's work, and his object seems to have been to assail its pessimistic message that scientific and technological progress lead to ruin.[1] To this end he constructed a counter-Atlantis, a fabulous island in the Pacific where science and technology had advanced centuries beyond what was known in Bacon's time but the citizens of which nevertheless retained their devout, friendly and law-abiding nature. Their exemplary behavior, unspoiled by ever increasing wealth and scientific knowledge, were Bacon's answer to Plato's pessimism.

Bacon's work thus both imitating and contradicting Plato's, it is an extraordinary coincidence that Bacon's ends, like Plato's, with the appearance of incompleteness but that, where the ending of the *Timaeus-Critias* is punitive, the *New-Atlantis* ends on a note of reward. Just as Critias's monologue ceases in the middle of a sentence and of the story, the account of Bacon's narrator, one of a crew of European sailors who have taken refuge in this new Atlantis, called Bensalem, ends with his description of the island society apparently still in progress, with no indication of whether or how the sailors returned home, with no hint of how the account reached Europe, and with no apparent reason why it should have broken off where it does. But in contrast to the δίκη which the disapproving gods, assembled at the center of the universe, are about to inflict on Atlantis as Critias falls silent, Bacon's narrator ends on a note of approval and reward. The father of Salomon's House, the research institute of the island, has just finished describing its purpose, works, and rites.

> And when he had said this he stood up; and I, as I had been taught,
> knelt down; and he laid his right hand upon my head, and said,

---

[1] Bacon, V, 347-413. The late Prof. Leo Strauss first called my attention to this little work.

'God bless thee, my son, and God bless this relation which I have made. I give thee leave to publish it, for the good of other nations; for we here are in God's bosom, a land unknown.' And so he left me; having assigned a value of about two thousand ducats for a bounty to me and my fellows. For they give great largesses, where they come, upon all occasions.

Thus both in the work as a whole and in its ending Bacon imitates a prominent aspect of Plato's story—the fabulous, technologically advanced island, the appearance of incompleteness—but contradicts the accompanying moral—prosperity instead of ruin, reward instead of punishment.[2] One might well conclude that Bacon set out to refute Plato as much as possible in Plato's own terms. If such is the case, then the seeming incompleteness of the *New Atlantis* is obviously feigned.

This is not the place to examine that possibility in detail. It is perhaps a straw in the wind that the time covered by the narrator's account appears to be twenty-one days, exactly half of the forty-two days which the authorities set as the limit of the crew's stay;[3] this suggests careful calculation of the mode and moment of conclusion rather than fortuitous interruption or abandonment. Furthermore, it would be hard to conceive of a grander climax for an early seventeenth-century work than the father's account of the wonders achieved by Salomon's House—the telescope, the microscope, the loud speaker and the hearing aid, flying machines, submarines, new varieties and species of plants and animals, artificial gases, artificial flavoring, and artificial climate.[4] There are, lastly, several suggestions of finality in the anomalous ending: at the beginning of his monologue the father lists a program of four topics which he will discuss, and at the end he has finished the

---

[2] It is true, of course, that at the end of Plato's work it is Atlantis which is punished, while at the end of Bacon's it is the visitors to Bensalem who are rewarded. The correlation is rather between the scenes of punishment and largesse with which the works end and, since the father of Salomon's House approaches the status of deity (pp. 395-397, 413), between divine punishment and divine reward.

[3] Bacon, V, 368. The limit is flexible, however (pp. 368, 385). Bacon's regular noting of the passage of time, as in a ship's log, is very marked. Although at some points there is a little uncertainty (pp. 385, 390, 391), twenty-one seems the most likely total. It is curious that there is an element of both precision and flexibility in both the time allowed and the time described.

[4] Bacon, V, 398-409.

fourth (his last paragraph begins "lastly"); [5] the final scene is
ceremonial and consists of elements well consorting with an ending—a blessing, an imprimatur, the cryptic revelation that the
island is "in God's bosom"; the father leaves; the giving of a
bounty, the rewarding of a task well done or a test well met as the
giver departs, has the ring of cadence. Bacon was no stranger to
the practice of esoteric writing; it is at least possible, and to me it
seems more likely than not, that he feigned the incompleteness of
the *New Atlantis*. [6]

But did he understand that the incompleteness of the *Timaeus-
Critias* was feigned? This does not necessarily follow from his
own artifice—he may simply have wanted the appearance of his
work to mirror that of Plato's—and yet it is hard to believe that
he would have feigned incompleteness himself without suspecting
that Plato feigned it too. Being of the opinion that in doubtful
matters such as this it is safer to believe that men of exceptional
intelligence saw what we can see than that they did not, I think
it likely that Bacon had at least some inkling of what Plato meant
by the form and manner of his ending. To that extent he is my
precursor.

---

[5] Bacon, V, 398.

[6] The profusion of numbers throughout the work suggests a numerological
element. Of the crew of fifty-one men seventeen are ill (p. 365). From this
datum and the number of single and double rooms provided by the Ben-
salemites the reader can calculate that the ship's complement consisted of
seven principal and forty-four subordinate men. The status of the narrator
is a similar riddle; he seems to be the principal man but one.

Bacon's chaplain and secretary, Rawley, who prepared the first edition
of his works, prefaced the *New Atlantis* with a note explaining the circumstances of its having been left incomplete, and appended to the work the
notice, "The rest was not perfected." Although this evidence must be allowed
considerable weight, it cannot be conclusive, since Rawley may not have been
privy to Bacon's intentions and, if not, probably never considered the
alternative explanation of seeming incompleteness.

WORKS CITED BY AUTHOR, EDITOR,
OR COMMENTATOR ONLY

Alline, H. A., *Histoire du texte de Platon*, Paris, 1915.
Aristophanes, *Nubes*, ed. L. L. Forman, New York and Cincinnati, 1915 (Forman).

Bacon, F., *Works*, ed. J. Spedding, R. Ellis, D. Heath, Boston, 1860-64.
Bowra, C. M., *Greek Lyric Poetry*, Oxford, ²1961.
Bramwell, J., *Lost Atlantis*, London, 1937.
Bruns, I., *Das literarische Porträt der Griechen im fünften und vierten Jahrhundert vor Christi Geburt*, Berlin, 1896.
Burnet, J., *Early Greek Philosophy*, London, ⁴1930 (EGP).
——, *Greek Philosophy*, Thales to Plato, London, 1914 (GP).

Chalcidius, *Platonis Timaeus interprete Chalcidio cum eiusdem commentario*, ed. J. Wrobel, Leipzig, 1876.
Cherniss, H., *The Riddle of the Early Academy*, Berkeley and Los Angeles, 1945.
Cornford, F., *Plato's Cosmology*, London, 1937.

Davies, J. K., *Athenian Propertied Families*, Oxford, 1971.

Forman (see Aristophanes).
Friedländer, P., *Plato*, Princeton, 1969 (first German edition, Berlin, 1928-30).

Gattefossé, J., and Roux, C., *Bibliographie de l'Atlantide*, Lyon, 1926.
Gauss, H., *Philosophischer Handkommentar zu den Dialogen Platons*, Bern, 1952-61.
Gomme, A. W., *A Historical Commentary on Thucydides*, Oxford, 1945-70.
Greene (see *Scholia Platonica*).
Guthrie, W. K. C., *A History of Greek Philosophy*, Cambridge, 1962-69.

Hackforth, R., "The Story of Atlantis, Its Purpose and Moral," *Classical Review* 58 (1944), 7-9.

Kirchner, J. E., *Prosopographia Attica*, Berlin, 1901-03.
Kirk, W., "Protagoras and Phaedrus, Literary Techniques," in *Studies Presented to D. M. Robinson*, ed. G. E. Mylonas and D. Raymond, St. Louis, 1953, II, 593-601.

Levinson, R. B., *In Defense of Plato*, Cambridge (Mass.), 1953.
Luce, J. V., *The End of Atlantis*, St. Albans, ²1970 (1st ed. 1969).

Martin, T. H., *Études sur le Timée de Platon*, Paris, 1841.

Philip, J. A., "The Platonic Corpus," *Phoenix* 24 (1970), 296-308.
Plato, *Timaeus and Critias*, trans. by A. E. Taylor, London, 1929 (Taylor TC).
Platon, *Timée, Critias*, texte établi et traduit par A. Rivaud, Paris, 1925 (Rivaud TC).

Procli Diodochi, *In Platonis Timaeum commentaria*, ed. E. Diehl, Leipzig, 1906 (Proclus).

Rivaud, A., "Platon auteur dramatique," *Revue d' histoire de la philosophie* 1 (1927), 125-51 (Rivaud *PAD*).
Rivaud *TC* (see Platon).
Rohde, E., "Γέγονε in den Biographica des Suidas," *RhM* 33 (1878), 161-220.
Rosenmeyer, T. G., "The Family of Critias," *AJP* 70 (1949), 404-10 (Rosenmeyer *FC*).
——, "Plato's Atlantis Myth: Timaeus or Critias?", *Phoenix* 10 (1956), 163-72 (Rosenmeyer *PAM*).

Scholia Platonica, ed. G. C. Greene, Haverford, 1938 (Greene).
Shorey, P., *What Plato Said*, Chicago, 1934.

Taylor *TC* (see Plato).
Taylor, A., *A Commentary on Plato's Timaeus*, Oxford, 1928 (Taylor *Comm*).

Welliver, W., *Questions of Intent*, Indianapolis, 1961 (privately published); dissertation, Univ. of Chicago, 1966; page citations refer to the latter.
West, M. L., *Iambi et Elegi Graeci*, Oxford, 1971.
Wilamowitz-Moellendorff, U. v., *Platon*, Berlin, ³1962 (first edition 1919).

Printed in the United States
By Bookmasters